AMERICAN INDIAN ART

NEW SHORTER EDITION

AMERICAN INDIAN ART

TEXT BY

NORMAN FEDER

HARRY N. ABRAMS, INC., PUBLISHERS, NEW YORK

FRONTISPIECE

1. Headdress. Tlingit or Haida. 7 x 5¾".
Denver Art Museum (Cat. No. QBC–2).
Collected by Ed Malin from the Kwakiutl,
but not of Kwakiutl manufacture.

Consulting Editor

DOUGLAS NEWTON

Curator, The Museum of Primitive Art, New York

Library of Congress Cataloging in Publication Data

Feder, Norman.
      American Indian art.

      Abridged paperback ed.
      Bibliography: p.
      1. Indians of North America—Art.   I.   Title
[E98.A7F38   1973]   709´.01´1   73-4857

Acknowledgments

So many people helped in the preparation of this book, and in so many different ways, that it is difficult to single out just a few for special mention. My main debt is certainly to the many museums and private collectors who not only had the forethought to amass and preserve their invaluable collections, but who also made their holdings available to me for study. I am deeply grateful to the staff members of these various institutions for their time, courtesy, and patience. In addition to locating specific treasures in their storerooms, they also searched through records for additional data, and in many cases even supervised photography. To all, my very sincere thanks.

Special acknowledgment must be given to Mr. Milford G. Chandler, certainly one of the most thorough collectors of all time, who unselfishly shared his deep insights of both Indian life and art, and who guided my appreciation of many little-known aspects of material culture.

I am indebted to Mr. Bill Holm of the Washington State Museum for reading the section pertaining to the Northwest Coast, and for making several very helpful suggestions.

Unfortunately most photographers remain anonymous, but I must single out Mr. Lloyd Rule of Denver who worked long hours taking nearly all the photographs of specimens in the Denver Art Museum. Special thanks also to Mr. Carmelo Guadagno of the Museum of the American Indian who supplied all of the photos from that institution.

And to the staff of the Denver Art Museum and particularly its director, Dr. Otto Karl Bach, for constant encouragement and inspiration, I express my deep gratitude.

The following private collectors and museum personnel have been particularly helpful:

Mr. L. Drew Bax, Mr. Larry Frank, Dr. William L. Gannon, Mr. John Hauberg, Dr. James Howard, Mr. Dennis Lessard, Mr. Richard Pohrt, and Mr. Roy H. Robinson.

Dr. Stanley A. Freed, American Museum of Natural History, New York

Mrs. Jane Powell Rosenthal, Brooklyn Museum, New York

Mr. Donald J. Metzger and Mr. Don W. Dragoo, Carnegie Museum, Pittsburgh

Mr. William Marshall and Mrs. Sally Roedeck, Colorado State Historical
    Society, Denver

Dr. Warren L. Wittry, Cranbrook Institute of Science, Bloomfield Hills, Michigan

Dr. Donald Collier, Dr. Philip H. Lewis, and Dr. Leon Siroto, Field
    Museum of Natural History, Chicago

Mr. Robert Hart and Mr. Myles Libhart, Indian Arts and Crafts Board,
    Washington, D.C.

Dr. Thomas A. Witty, Kansas State Museum, Topeka

Dr. Robert Ritzenthaler, Milwaukee Public Museum, Wisconsin

Dr. Alan R. Woolworth, Minnesota Historical Society, St. Paul

Dr. Frederick J. Dockstader and Mr. William F. Stiles, Museum of the
    American Indian, New York

Mr. Douglas Newton and Mr. Allan Chapman, Museum of Primitive Art, New York

Dr. Dave Damas, National Museum of Canada, Ottawa

Mr. Marvin F. Kivett, Nebraska Historical Society, Lincoln

Dr. William N. Fenton and Mr. Charles E. Gillette, New York State Museum, Albany

Mrs. Mahala E. Mueller, Northern Plains Indian Crafts Association,
    Billings, Montana

Dr. Ernest S. Dodge, Peabody Museum, Salem, Massachusetts

Mr. Charles F. Hayes III, Rochester Museum of Arts and Science, New York

Dr. Edward S. Rogers and Mr. Harold Burnham, Royal Ontario Museum, Toronto

Mr. Roy E. Coy, St. Joseph Museum, Missouri

Mr. Charles R. DeBusk and Miss Lillian R. Smith, Sioux City Public Museum, Iowa

Mr. Carl Dentzel and Mr. Bruce Brian, Southwest Museum, Los Angeles

Dr. Saul H. Riesenberg, Dr. William Sturtevant, Mrs. Margaret Blaker,
    and Mr. Robert Elder, United States National Museum, Smithsonian
    Institution, Washington, D.C.

Miss Frances Eyman and Mr. David Crownover, University Museum, Philadelphia

Dr. Joan Freeman, State Historical Society of Wisconsin, Madison

N. F.

Denver, 1965

Contents

List of Plates

Whenever possible, museum catalogue numbers have been included in the plate captions.

Colorplates are indicated by an asterisk (*).

AREAS
OF
INDIAN CULTURES
IN
NORTH AMERICA

Introduction

The past decade has seen an increasing awareness of American Indian art develop among the American people. A short twenty-five years ago, the only place where primitive art could be seen was in the usual culturally oriented exhibits of the major natural history museums. Today, such museums have begun to display specimens with an emphasis on their artistic qualities, and art museums are forming new departments of primitive art. In addition, certain types of American Indian materials are in demand by discriminating collectors as well as by museums.

It is somewhat difficult to explain this sudden interest in American Indian art, but it is probably due to at least two major factors. First of all, the general increased awareness of the arts of Africa and Oceania, owing in part to the enthusiasm of modern artists in Europe, has tended to draw attention to the arts of America. In other words, American Indian art is riding on the popularity bandwagon of a widespread interest in primitive art from all regions of the world.

Another factor is that the American Indians are gradually being assimilated into American society. This is partly due to government programs of termination and relocation, and partly to an inevitable process of acculturation which began with the Indians' first contact with Europeans, and has been going on ever since. At this point we can look into the future and foresee the final stage of this process: almost complete acculturation will have taken place, resulting, of course, in the complete disappearance of the native arts.

Interest in, and collection of, American Indian art has gone through a series of phases. During the first hundred years of the discovery of this art, examples of Indian handcraft were eagerly sought as souvenirs, and were taken or sent back to Europe as specimens of the strange and wonderful things being produced by the American natives. This interest lasted into the second half of the nineteenth century in some areas of the Plains.

With further contact, the early sense of novelty wore off; on the one hand, Indians were usually hated or ignored by those who lived in proximity to them, while on the other, people remote from the Indians developed overly romantic notions about them based on the novels of James Fenimore Cooper and Karl May. This latter group continued to collect as the opportunity afforded itself.

The final phase is the present one. Collecting is again feverish, a last effort to obtain whatever is left of the old culture before it completely disappears.

11

2. Large pottery bowl. Zuñi. Diameter 28″. Denver Art Museum (Cat. No. X–Zu–46–P). The deer with heart lines are a common Zuñi motif.

In spite of the fact that Indian exhibits have been on view in American museums at least since 1800, and at present there is an interest in collecting artifacts, even today only a small portion of the vast variety of Indian production is deemed worthy of display. The implication is that only a modest segment of this production has any artistic merit. The usual display of American Indian art found in an American museum tends to rely heavily on prehistoric material, an emphasis which is carried over into the few books on the subject. Typically, these exhibits include several examples of Northwest Coast wood carving, a painted shield and buffalo robe from the Plains, and perhaps a fetish and *kachina* from the Southwest. Nevertheless, the art of the historic American Indians has a great deal more to offer than the few examples currently valued by collectors. One of the main reasons why more Indian material is not displayed is sheer lack of knowledge of the variety of Indian production.

The acceptance of Indian art by the general public is directly related to efforts to popularize it by exhibits and publications. These efforts started in 1931 with the Exposition of Indian Tribal Arts, advertised as "the first exhibition of American Indian art selected entirely with consideration of aesthetic value."[1] This was followed in 1939 by a major show at the San Francisco World's Fair organized by Frederic H. Douglas and René d'Harnoncourt, who later created a similar exhibit at the Museum of Modern Art in New York in 1941. The book *Indian Art of the United States*, a collaboration between Douglas and d'Harnoncourt and based on the New York exhibition, has become a classic on the subject. In 1949 and in 1950 two important books[2] devoted solely to the art of the Northwest Coast area assured recognition for this art form. Subsequent exhibits and publications on specific aspects of Indian art—sculpture, paintings, ceramics—have all made their contribution to the popularization of the subject. In all probability, if there were a major exhibition focusing on some special aspect of Indian art, such as Woodland wooden dolls or Plains sculptured catlinite pipes, these artifacts would come to enjoy the same popularity as those which are already well known, such as Northwest Coast art.

INDIAN ART

The area of America which lies north of Mexico is vast, and the people native to each of the sections of this territory differ notably from each other physically, linguistically, and culturally. Yet, by popular usage, all are called Indians, or Eskimos in the far northern sections. This has led to the fairly widespread misconception that all Indians are alike, and generalizations concerning Indian art are common. In reality, it is almost impossible to make generalizations which genuinely apply to this whole vast region.

Each tribal group—in some instances even each division of a tribal group—should be considered as a separate entity. However, since there are no less than over three hundred different tribes, anthropologists have been forced to utilize the concept of "culture areas" as a convenient tool for discussions of groups which are culturally similar. This concept is adopted here for its practical value.

Tribal styles within any one culture area may vary, and are usually quite distinct; culture areas and artistic areas, in fact, do not necessarily correspond. For instance, even the least trained eye will notice that the colors, designs, and techniques of application are completely different in Crow and Cheyenne decorative beadwork although both tribes are located in the Plains culture area. Some of these tribal differences will be discussed in the section on culture areas.

USE OF MATERIALS AND TECHNIQUES

As a rule, the Indian artist generally used whatever material was most readily available: wood and wood products were the dominant materials in the Northwest Coast and Woodland areas, buffalo hides on the Plains, and clay in the Southwest. However, almost everywhere the rare material was eagerly sought because of the prestige its ownership brought. The intertribal trade in finished products was paralleled by the trade in raw materials, and long journeys were undertaken to obtain them. Seashells from the Pacific were traded as far east as the upper Missouri River area, and were common in the Southwest. Parrot feathers, metal bells, and seashells were traded into the Southwest from central Mexico. Catlinite for pipe bowls was traded from a center at Pipestone, Minnesota throughout all the Plains area as far as the

13

3. Beaded moccasins. Iowa. c. 1860. Length 10¾″. Collection Milford G. Chandler, Detroit. A fine example of the colorful abstract style which developed near the Kansas–Nebraska border.

state of Washington. Skins, horns, bowwoods, and pigments were also commonly traded.

The use of any given material, then, is not necessarily indicative of its place of origin. Furthermore, the distribution of some materials has changed with time, particularly in the case of animal sources. The bison, for example, once widespread over the Plains and parts of the Woodland area as well, are now confined to national parks. Other creatures—the Plains grizzly, the ivory-billed woodpecker, and the Carolina parakeet—at one time fairly plentiful over a wide area, are now all but extinct.

The wide variety of materials introduced by Europeans in some instances had a radical effect, being readily accepted by the Indians as more colorful than native equivalents, or better suited to their purposes. Originally they were supplied as gifts to win Indian friendship and alliance. This was particularly true in the days when Europeans were a minority, but also during the days when England, France, Spain, Sweden, and Holland were all vying with one another for control of territory. The custom of gift-giving lasted well through the period of the American Revolution and was gradually replaced by the trade in furs. (Some individuals, like John Jacob Astor of the American Fur Company, controlled large portions of the fur trade and became the first American self-made millionaires.) An extensive industry was developed to supply goods which would entice the Indians to deal with a specific merchant. Many silversmiths, at first in England, and later in New York, Philadelphia, Detroit, and Montreal were kept busy producing ornaments for Indians instead of table services for Europeans.

European manufactures even duplicated Indian crafts on a mass production basis. If the Indian valued such things as wampum beads laboriously handmade of clam shells, Europeans would and did manufacture them in quantity for Indian trade. Others, finding the wampum industry too difficult or costly, had special imitation wampum made of glass beads. Likewise dentalium shells were supplied by traders throughout the Plains, and abalone shells were traded into the Southwest.

Indian trading posts are still a common feature of the American economy but, of course, they are small businesses compared to the Astor era. Modern traders supply glass beads, shells, wool cloths, brass bells, dyed feathers, and a host of other raw materials used by present-day Indians in their craftwork. The romantic purist today bemoans the fact that traders stock brightly colored—often garish—materials, but neglects the fact that these items please Indian taste. The older, softer, pastel shades produced with native dyes were eagerly replaced with aniline dyes. Improved methods of coloring glass also had a profound effect on Indian arts, usually one which was less pleasing to non-Indian taste. A very few traders, in the interest of modern commercial production, have persuaded Indians to use again the older native dyes (as in the case of some Navaho rugs), or have specially ordered glass beads in the older, subdued colors. However, in general, Indians will not employ either for their own use.

CHANGE VERSUS STABILITY

Almost everywhere, American Indians were firmly confined within the conventional artistic limits imposed by their particular society. The individual artist was usually allowed very little freedom of expression, though the degree varied from tribe to tribe. Objects connected with religion were usually more conventionalized than secular items, so that various examples of the Hemis *kachina* mask made by the Hopi look very much the same regardless of who made them. A few minor changes resulted from the introduction of new,

15

better, or more colorful materials. However, while a newer paint pigment might be substituted for an older, native one, the painted area and design usually remained the same.[3] Major changes in style or material were infrequent and often the result of more or less accidental influences. Examples of such innovations were the black pottery developed by Maria Martinez at San Ildefonso, or the Haida carvings in argillite. But these were unusual developments.[4]

A variety of factors have brought about gradual changes in American Indian Art: intertribal trade as a factor in spreading tribal art styles (definitely one of the major causes of radical changes), the introduction of new materials, and the adaptation of European patterns and designs into Indian crafts. Such adaptations as silver brooches, hair plates, and earrings were introduced first as gifts and were later copied by the Indians themselves. Probably at first the Indians copied these non-Indian examples in as minute detail as their tools would allow, but a gradual process of experimentation with new forms, and new techniques for applying designs ultimately developed to the point where each tribe had formed some unique stylistic formula. The "chip carving-like" effect produced by filing with a metal file, used by the Winnebago on their metal bracelets, is an outstanding example of technique and design style of Indian invention applied to a basically non-Indian product.

There is still controversy among students of Indian material culture about the origin of such traits as, for example, the floral designs used in much Woodland beadwork. Are these copies of embroideries taught in French mission schools, or did the Indian receive his inspiration for floral designs from seeing European garments so decorated? To state it another way, it is possible that entire design concepts were introduced by Europeans and readily accepted by Indians over a wide area. Also, the origin of the shape of the Indian crooked knives is a debatable point, and so is the question of whether the technique for making finger-woven yarn sashes in a multiple braiding is aboriginal or introduced. Some of these problems will never be resolved, but it is certain that introduced materials and designs had a tremendous impact on aboriginal crafts.

One common cause of radical change occurs with the development of a new religion. Among American Indian groups a new religion usually started with an individual having a dream-revelation in which he received full instructions concerning ritual and the religious equipment necessary to it. The ritual and equipment might often be based on some older form, but were frequently complete innovations. Such new religions have created objects like the Ghost Dance painted shirts, the specific form of decoration on Dream Dance drums, the Three Dweller dolls of the Eastern Sioux, and the distinctive form of Kickapoo prayer sticks.

Often a dream-revelation was an individual experience which dictated

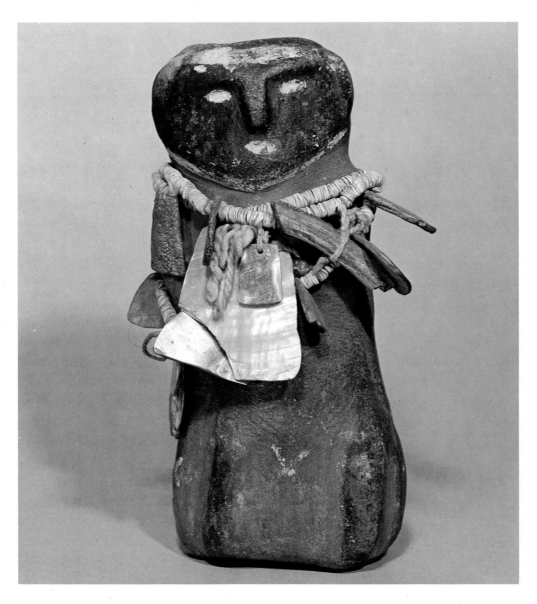

4. Painted stone fetish. Zia Pueblo. 7⅞ x 3½″. Denver Art Museum (Cat. No. QZ–1)

the design a man painted on his shield, the ornaments he chose to wear in his hair, or the way in which he painted his face. Sometimes these designs were perpetuated by gift or purchase, especially if their magical power proved effective. However, they were as frequently discarded upon the death of the originator.

We have mentioned that, in general, items connected with religion became the most standardized and least subject to change within the originating tribe. However, when a given piece of religious equipment passed from one tribe to another it almost always suffered a series of changes which were often radical. In fact, an object which was sacred in the originating tribe was often secularized within the borrowing tribe. One example which will make this clear is the spread of *tablita* dances from the Rio Grande Pueblos to the Hopi. Among Rio Grande groups, during a dance variously called the Corn or the Harvest Dance, the women wear very simple and small *tablitas* (small board headdresses), the form and shape of which have probably not changed materially for at least a hundred years. However, when a similar dance was introduced to the Hopi as the Butterfly Dance, they began an elaboration of the basic *tablita* form into large and involved shapes with ample painting in polychrome. These are still being produced in elaborate forms, and individual makers have a tremendous amount of freedom in design. This presents a marked contrast to the rigid conventions followed by the Hopi in making their sacred *kachina* masks, or among Rio Grande *tablita* makers. Needless to say, among the Hopi the Butterfly Dance is considered more secular than sacred.

Change also occurs quite frequently with the breakdown of old established religions and military societies. Suddenly items which were once sacred become secular, and their forms become more subject to alteration. Dream Dance drums, which are considered highly sacred by tribal groups practicing the Drum religion, are used as powwow drums or even coffee tables by groups which no longer practice this religion. Standardized ritual equipment and costumes of a particular military society are altered and used indiscriminately by anyone after the society breaks down. This occurred frequently throughout the Plains after the Indians were placed on reservations, and the opportunity for warfare was no longer present. As the military societies became obsolete, their ritual equipment was stored away in old trunks. Years later, with the reintroduction of the Grass Dance and the popularity of the intertribal powwow, youngsters wanting to dance would rummage through grandfather's trunk for anything which they might wear as a dancing costume. Of course, they found old society regalia and, not knowing the significance of these items, wore them for their Grass dancing. Others seeing these old items being worn, copied them in slightly altered form, and as a result, new styles were developed.

In the Oklahoma area and elsewhere, a special phenomenon known as Pan-Indianism[5] has developed. Here many different tribes were placed on reservations in proximity to one another, and a blending and borrowing of tribal styles evolved to the point where most groups completely lost their individuality. Today in Oklahoma, instead of distinct Ponca, Oto, Osage, Pawnee, Cheyenne, and Kiowa styles, there is one common Oklahoma style with only occasional tribal differences still visible. This blending is particularly evident among the male population. American Indian women are almost universally more conservative than the men, and it is still possible, even in Oklahoma, to identify a woman's tribe by some distinctive article of her dress. Often the women continue to wear a particular tribal style of moccasins, or the cut of their blouses remains unchanged. Some women seem to take a certain amount of pride in their conservatism of dress, but some styles of women's clothing are worn for their prestige value in preference to

18

the older tribal styles. In Oklahoma, for example, women of any tribe will wear the buckskin beaded dresses in Cheyenne style if they can possibly obtain them. This dress has become the standard Pan-Indian powwow style because it is made of Indian tanned buckskin, which is hard to obtain, and because it has a considerable amount of beaded decoration, which makes it comparatively expensive. Rarity and high cost have made this dress a symbol of prestige.

To sum up, it is fairly safe to state that change is a continual but slow processs interrupted only very rarely by a radical innovation. For example, in comparing Sioux Indian pipe bags manufactured in 1850 with pipe bags made in 1900 and 1950 respectively, one can see considerable variations in decorative designs, techniques, and materials. However, the basic form of the bag remains much the same throughout all of this hundred-year period. A comparison of Sioux pipe bags manufactured over a segment of this period—say in 1900, 1905, and 1910—would show hardly any major alterations whatever, although some slight variations would probably be present.

THE INDIAN ARTIST

Among American Indians, specialization of labor was the exception rather than the rule, and each family was generally a self-sufficient unit. At times, particular large-scale undertakings, such as the Plains Indian buffalo drives, or the Pueblo cleaning of the irrigation ditches, called for community effort. But if isolated from the rest of their community, a husband and wife team could produce for themselves almost everything necessary for their survival. The outstanding exception was the specialization of some select individuals in the healing arts; however, even these doctors, *shamans*, or medicine men still had to be self-sufficient since the fees for their services were rarely enough to support them adequately.

There was usually a division of craftwork by sex. In areas where hunting constituted a major part of the economy, the males concentrated on producing equipment for the hunt, and a major portion of their time was spent in the chase. In these groups, most of the other necessary household crafts fell to the females. For example, in most of the Plains area, the men made bows and arrows, some horse gear, shields, and charms connected with warfare, and a limited amount of religious equipment. At the same time, the women made the domestic equipment, clothing, utensils (such as *parfleche* containers), and carried out all the beading and quilling for decoration on garments and ceremonial items.

Among the Pueblo groups which depended on agriculture, the men were the farmers. Hunting was still men's work, but it was such a secondary part of the economy that it occupied little of their time. The men, therefore, also practiced such crafts as weaving which was often the work of women in other societies. The women in Pueblo groups made pottery, basketwork, and carried out general domestic chores.

The upper Missouri earth-lodge people, and most Woodland groups, had an economy about equally divided between agriculture and the hunt, and among them the women were the farmers and the men the hunters. In a few areas some forms of specialization did occur. Perhaps the most notable was in the Northwest Coast where certain individuals were famous for their skill as wood-carvers and were commissioned to make important carvings.

While it is generally true that all Pueblo women could and did make pottery, or that all Plains men could make bows and arrows, or that all Sioux women could decorate a pair of moccasins with beadwork, it was also an accepted fact that—without being actual specialists—certain individuals were known for their exceptional ability in a specific craft. Thus some men, noted for their skill in chipping arrowpoints, would aften produce more points than they needed for their own use, and would then barter their surplus to a ready market. Almost everywhere fine craftsmanship was recognized by the population at large, and skilled artisans gained prestige through their labors. This was perhaps carried to an extreme among the Cheyenne where a special women's society was organized solely to produce sacred items. This Guild of Southern Cheyenne Women[6] had an organization in many respects parallel to that of men's military societies. The women recognized as the best bead workers within the tribe would meet together to make tepees, tepee linings, pillows, and bed sheets all in a standard form. Various members of the guild would proudly recount the number of linings they had beaded, much in the way a man would recount his war exploits.

Specialization was also connected with non-essential crafts. Only a few individuals within each tribe became proficient in the production of silver ornaments, and they were easily able to produce enough to satisfy the demands of their entire tribe. This same sort of specialization is common today, but with items, once essential, which have since been replaced with articles of non-Indian manufacture. While it was once important for every woman to be able to make moccasins for her family, her family now wears commercially manufactured shoes for normal wear. Traditional Indian moccasins are still worn to a limited extent during some religious observances and at intertribal powwows but, on a day-to-day basis, the demand is not on the great scale of the past. Therefore, only a few women, recognized as experts, still manufacture moccasins to supply the limited demand. The same can be said for most items of traditional Indian craft which are still in limited use; only a comparatively few women have the knowledge and willingness to tan hides, to decorate with porcupine quillwork, to make a *parfleche*, or to weave a basket.

20

INDIAN ART
by Culture Areas

While I have previously mentioned that the "culture area" concept is admittedly not ideal in discussing stylistic areas, it is, nevertheless, in such common usage that I employ it here as a basic guide to the art regions. However, I will discuss separately the major styles with only a brief introduction to the socio-economic definition of each area.[7]

5. Bear mask. Haida (?). Carnegie Museum, Pittsburgh. Fred Harvey Collection (Cat. No. 3178/28)

6. House partition screen. Tlingit. Height 15′. Denver Art Museum (Cat. No. QT1–41). The famous bear screen, once the property of Chief Shakes of Wrangell, Alaska.

The Plains

THE PLAINS

The Plains comprises the territory from the Rocky Mountains to the Mississippi Valley and from Texas and Oklahoma north into Canada. The inhabitants depended mainly upon the bison for food, clothing, shelter, and other necessities of life, though in parts of the Plains some agriculture was practiced and bison hunting became a seasonal activity. These Plains people are the ones most commonly thought of as being "typically Indian" in that they were the warriors who fought Custer, wore feather bonnets, and lived in skin tepees. Elaborately decorated skin clothing was common but, in general, material possessions were few because of the nomadic existence necessitated by following the bison herds.

The Plains culture pattern was dependent upon the horse for its development. Prior to the introduction of this animal, the Plains area was only sparsely settled by semi-sedentary groups that practiced some agriculture in addition to sporadic hunting. Horses, of course, were introduced by Europeans, most probably the early Spanish explorers in the Southwest. The horse gave the Indian in this area the mobility needed to hunt the bison successfully, and to transport his tent and personal belongings. The other salient features of Plains culture are the importance of warfare, which was the accepted method of gaining prestige, and the annual religious ceremony known as the Sun Dance.

From an artistic standpoint the Plains is not a homogeneous area. Certain traits are common throughout the entire region, but even these are generally stylistically distinguishable. For examples, most Plains tribes produce skin garments and horse trappings elaborately decorated with bead or porcupine quill embroidery, but each tribe that does so uses distinct designs and techniques. Likewise most Plains groups produce the painted rawhide containers known as *parfleches*, painted shields, painted tepees, robes, and tepee linings with pictographic designs, carved stone pipes, feather bonnets, and some metalwork. Certain other crafts such as ribbon appliqué for decoration, carved wooden bowls and war clubs, and yarn bags and belts are only found in parts of the area.

During the first half of the nineteenth century, most of the Plains area was uninhabited by Europeans, and as a result very little pre-1850 Plains material is now extant. Hence little is known about early Plains styles. The earliest collectors in the Plains area included Prince Maximilian and George Catlin, both in the 1830s. Other small collections were made by military expeditions such as those of Lewis and Clark, and Nathan Sturges Jarvis at Fort Snelling. These people all collected mainly on the eastern fringes of the Plains area, and used the Mississippi or the Missouri rivers as the main routes for their travel. Catlin actually made a trip into the Southern Plains area, but unfortunately was ill most of the while. As a result we have almost no documented early material from the Southern Plains, and very little from the Central Plains.

The early Plains material which has survived seems to indicate that even in the pre-1850 period Plains people were prone to elaborate decoration of garments with beads or quills, with a considerable use of split bird quills instead of the more usual porcupine quills. Bird quillwork is not adequately described in the literature, and just what species was utilized is not known. A limited amount of work in bird quills was still being produced in the Fort Berthold area as late as 1900, but this now seems obsolete in the Plains. Only a few Northern Athabascans in Canada and some Eskimo continue to use a limited amount of bird quills for decoration.

Another characteristic of early Plains quillwork is the substitution of the stems of the maidenhair fern (*Adiantum*) for porcupine quill whenever black was desired. Evidently Indians west of the Mississippi did not know the secret of how to dye quills black until after contact with the white man, although Eastern Indians used black dyed quills in place of maidenhair fern stems. It is, therefore, fairly easy to determine if a piece of pre-1850 quillwork is from the Plains or the Woodland area. In general, Plains people used only the natural white, yellow, orange red, and dark brown maidenhair fern stems in their quillwork, while Eastern Indians were able to obtain bright reds and blacks.

Early in the nineteenth century, the fur traders introduced wool cloth, called "stroud," in both red and blue, and these colors were often transferred to quills by boiling the quills and pieces of cloth together. Occasionally a purple could be made by combining the red and blue, and sometimes a weak green was obtained by combining the blue cloth dye with a natural yellow usually obtained from bloodroot (*Sanguinaria canadensis*). Whenever green is found in early Plains quillwork it is safe to presume that the quill is probably bird and not porcupine; the pithy inside of the bird quill was usually left intact in splitting the quill for use and this substance took a dye more readily than the hard-surfaced porcupine quill. A Cheyenne specialty, right up to the modern period, was the substitution of various grasses and, later, of corn husk for porcupine quills. Very little documented early porcupine quillwork came from the Northern Plains, and I do not know of a single early documented specimen from the Southern Plains. Porcupine quillwork decoration on buckskin, then, seems to have been confined to the groups along the upper Missouri and into the Central Plains area and may very well be the westward extension of an Eastern craft.

In the early part of the nineteenth century, beads were introduced into the Plains, and—although some quillwork has continued up to the present—beadwork soon began gradually to replace the older tradition. Early beads were fairly large, of a type known as "pony beads," and were mostly white, black, and blue, so that early Plains beadwork is characterized by bold designs in either blue and white or black and white. A major reason for the great use of these three colors is their relative cheapness to produce, which therefore afforded a greater margin of profit to the traders who carried them. Right up the the present day, with our improved methods of coloring glass, it is still more costly to produce beads in reds and yellows, while black and white remain the least expensive of all.

The smaller glass beads known as "seed beads" were in use in the Western Plains as early as 1830, and probably by that date the Western Plains Indians were in a position to obtain any of the usual trade items available to Eastern Indians of the period. When Astor withdrew from the fur trade in 1834, a host of independent traders entered the field and established a chain of trading posts all along the eastern foot of the Rockies. Keen competition must have forced these independent traders to stock a wide variety of goods.

When we consider the period after 1850, we are on much surer ground because of the vast bulk of artifacts collected and still in existence. Warfare between Indians and United States troops was at its peak during this period; soldiers often took souvenirs of battles, many of which are now on deposit with the United States National Museum (Smithsonian Institution) in Washington, D.C. By the late 1860s most of the Plains Indians were placed on reservations—a course which, while altering their way of life, also made Plains material plentiful for the collector. A careful analysis of this material reveals distinct styles and influences in many directions, both into and out of the Plains area.

The groups of the Central Plains, Sioux, Cheyenne, and Arapaho are considered most typical of the Plains area. They all produce quantities of beaded articles. The beads are sewn in the lazy-stitch and geometric designs.

The Sioux living in North and South Dakota are particularly fond of covering large areas with bead or quillwork, usually in not more than four or five different colors. The designs are often developed by combining triangles and straight lines. In contrast, the Crow of southern Montana use an overlay sewing technique. Their designs are very similar to, and perhaps derived from, those painted on their *parfleches*. These people are fond of using as many colors as possible—up to twenty or so—on a single item, and of having them all blend into a pleasing design. Still another characteristic of Crow beadwork is the technique of outlining a central design motif in white beads running in a different direction from the rows of background beadwork (color, plate 17). This style is not found among the Blackfeet, the northern neighbors of the Crow, or among the Sioux to the south; however, it has a wide distribution to the west and southwest from the Crow center. The Nez Percé in Idaho seem to have copied the Crow style with the greatest fidelity, and much Nez Percé beadwork is indistinguishable from that of the Crow (color, plate 18). Other typical Plateau groups such as the Yakima, Umatilla, and Walla Walla seem to have borrowed the style from the Nez Percé. From the Southwest come occasional examples of beadwork produced by the Shoshone and Ute, both of which bear a strong resemblance to the Crow style and were undoubtedly derived from it.

The Northern Plains, comprised of portions of northern North Dakota, Montana, and parts of southern Canada, evolved still another distinct substyle. Here the beadwork is in bold geometric designs with the beads applied in an overlay stitch in straight lines. There is a tendency to develop all the lines by using small solid rectangles joined from corner to corner. Most of the Northern Plains work is limited to four or five colors. The Blackfeet tribe is probably the center of this style today, but it may have originated, at some time in the past, through influences from the upper Missouri River tribes. The style extends among the Assiniboin and Montana Gros Ventre, the Yanktonai, and in slightly modified form, among the Sarcee and Plains Cree.

It might be well to mention here that another different and distinct style is also popular in the same area, in the form of an overlay beadwork in a floral motif. This style, introduced sometime before 1900, was widely distributed all across the Northern Plains, even reaching the Sioux and Crow. It certainly had its origin in the eastern area, and probably spread west across the Northern Plains with Plains Cree and Plains Ojibwa peoples. These two numerous tribes were great travelers, and probably carried the style clear up into the interior Athabascan tribes of Alaska. In Montana a group of these people settled on the Rocky Boy reservation near Havre, where they continue to influence neighboring tribes.

Another style is found in the Southern Plains area among the Kiowa, Comanche, and Southern Cheyenne tribes. Here bead decoration takes the form of light, delicate bead trim in contrast to the large bead-covered areas employed in the north. Shirts and leggings from this region usually lack the fully beaded strips on sleeves, shoulders, and down each legging. Women's dresses generally have only a simple band across the shoulders; the Cheyenne add an additional band on the front and back. These designs are normally simple geometric units done with only one row of the lazy-stitch on men's garments and with few colors—much like an overly simplified Sioux style. Moccasins, however, are normally fully beaded by the Cheyenne and sometimes by the Kiowa Indians as well. As a replacement for the elaborate beading, buckskin is often painted in yellow, blue, and green by the Kiowa and Comanche, and in red and yellow by the Cheyenne. In addition, Kiowa

28

and Comanche often cut long, and sometimes twisted, fine skin fringes.

The Kiowa are also noted for two other distinct forms of bead decoration. One is the use of an abstract floral type element. It is difficult to define, but distinct from floral styles found elsewhere, and is usually carried out in an overlay bead sewing technique (plate 9). The other distinct form is a peculiar bead sewing stitch which is actually a form of bead netting. Formerly it was used by the Kiowa and Comanche to decorate moccasins, baby carriers, and beaded pouches. It is now known as the "gourd" stitch or the "peyote" stitch because at present it is used by Indians everywhere to decorate the fans, staffs, and gourd rattles used in the Peyote ceremonies of the Native American Church. It is possible that these two styles were introduced to the Kiowa by displaced Delaware Indians from the East Coast. Delaware and some Shawnee had an abstract floral style much like that of the Kiowa, and both tribes used the gourd stitch in making garters and other ornaments. In addition, the Delaware were in the Texas area as early as 1820, when they came into contact with Kiowa as they still do today.

In the southwestern Plains live the Ute and Jicarilla Apache. The Ute were basically a mountain tribe which mainly lived by hunting deer and elk, and only seasonally ventured into the Plains proper in search of the bison. During the latter half of the nineteenth century, both tribes were pushed to the west side of the mountains by the pressure of Kiowa and Comanche raiding. They received some influence on their art from the Cheyenne who hunted in the same area, but much more must have come down through the mountains from the north, from the Crow through the intermediary, the Shoshone.

The Ute and Jicarilla both decorated their moccasins using typical Cheyenne designs; however, the Jicarilla cut their patterns in a unique way, with pointed toes and a slit down the instep. Some beading on pouches and horse trappings is very similar to the Crow style in having white-outlined overlay geometric designs in a variety of colors. In addition, these tribes developed a style that, while distinctively their own, is yet reminiscent of pre-1850 work from the Central Plains area. Working with the smaller seed beads, from about 1850 on, they produced leggings, shirt strips, and bands for women's dresses with massive triangular designs in two or three colors. Usually blue and white or black and white, the beadwork thus seems to be a continuation of the early widespread Plains style in pony beads. A somewhat similar survival of this old massive, basic color style was found on parts of the Plateau as late as the early part of this century.

The Ute and Jicarilla, unlike most other Plains tribes, produced a type of coiled basketry very similar to that of some Paiute, Navaho, and Pueblo groups at Jemez. In short, these two tribes incorporated in their art elements from each of the many tribes with which they came into contact.

On the eastern fringes of the Plains are several other distinct groups.

The upper Missouri River area is the home of the Mandan, Hidatsa, and Arikara, three separate tribes which now reside on the Fort Berthold reservation in North Dakota. These tribes were semi-sedentary; they lived in earth-lodges for the major portion of each year, and hunted bison only seasonally. Living along the Missouri River, these people utilized simple round skin-covered boats called "bull boats." Generally they were farmers. Their combination of farming and earth-lodge dwelling was evidently the common pattern over most of the Plains in the prehorse period. They made a little basketry and pottery. They produced the usual beaded and quilled buckskin garments in the style of the Northern Plains people (plate 11). The designs used most closely resemble those of the neighboring Northern Plains groups to the west; however, a mixed style developed due to influences from related tribes. For example, the Hidatsa and Crow were at one time a single tribe which split up sometime before the historic period. They speak closely related languages, and frequently visit and intermarry. Partly as a result, the Hidatsa have adopted many Crow design motifs. Likewise, the Arikara and Pawnee at one time belonged to a single tribe, and even today they share much in common.

The so-called Prairie tribes, to the south of the upper Missouri, form still another distinct artistic area. These groups, however, are also not very homogeneous and they could easily be broken into smaller art areas. Basically they differ from other Plains tribes in the larger number of Woodland traits which they have adopted. They make twined yarn bags and finger-woven sashes in the Woodland style, utilize cloth apparel decorated with ribbon appliqué or beadwork in an abstract floral style, and wear soft-sole moccasins in contrast to the usual Plains hard-sole types.

These groups tend to replace the Sun Dance with the Grand Medicine Society of the Great Lakes area. The Pawnee tribe living in Nebraska seems to have developed a most complex religious organization which had a profound influence on all their neighbors. However, the Pawnee apparently did not contribute much in the way of artistic styles.

It is difficult at this late date to try to reconstruct the locations of style centers and to trace the diffusion of any particular style from its center. However, I believe that a style center developed in the early reservation period around the southeastern portion of Nebraska and northeastern part of Kansas. Here the Iowa and Sauk-and-Fox of the Nemaha reservation, combined with the neighboring Oto and Missouri, seem to have developed a very rich form of decoration using the abstract floral beaded designs (plates 13, 14; color, plate 3). The Oto-Missouri were probably responsible for spreading this style to the Osage and Kaw as well as to the Omaha and Ponca. This same basic style was common among the Nebraska Winnebago and the Prairie Potawatomi in Kansas. Either or both could have played a large part in developing it. Certainly the basic idea of abstracting floral designs developed along the eastern part of the Kansas–Nebraska line, and the impetus must have come from an older floral style in the Great Lakes area. In all probability the Winnebago, Potawatomi, and Sauk-and-Fox brought a basic floral tradition with them when they moved to Kansas and Nebraska, and this changed upon contact with the Iowa and Oto-Missouri.

Painting, on a variety of objects, occupies a prominent place among Plains techniques. In precontact times, the Indians had only a limited range of natural pigments, including red and yellow ochers, a brown lignite, and perhaps a very limited amount of native blues and greens. Some of the oldest surviving painted buffalo hides seem to be done in brown only, with colorless glue sizing. The glue sizing lines did not show up at first on a freshly painted hide, but appeared white after the hide became dirty. At a very early date, a mercury vermilion from China was introduced by trade; consequently, hides from the first half of the nineteenth century were often painted in red, brown, and white. Still later, with the introduction of other commercial pigments, hides were also painted in green, blue, and yellow.

There seems to be little difference between hides from the Central Plains and the upper Missouri areas. The standard designs were a sunburst of concentric circles made up of feather-like elements (often called the "black bonnet" design), and a box-and-border design (color, plates 28, 29). The sunburst type seems to have been worn by men, while the box-and-border was worn by women; however, both styles were painted only by women. The many variations on these two basic patterns probably indicate local styles (plate 15). Southern Plains peoples, Kiowa and Comanche, painted a design of an hourglass with border. Blackfeet often painted hides with simple horizontal stripes.[8] Very early hides show the use of a border with a complex design in the center, but unfortunately the tribes they came from have not been identified.

Plainted shields are not easily assigned to areas because they vary considerably even within a single tribe. This of course was due to the fact that the shield type and design had been dictated by a vision. Generally the form of a shield was cut from the thick skin on the neck of a bison and shrunk so as to become convex. Sometimes it was painted, but more often a soft buckskin painted cover was fitted over the rawhide. Occasionally, still a third layer was added: an undecorated cover to protect the painted one. The Crow Indians in particular seem to have produced large numbers of shields. These are usually about twenty-two inches in diameter, have a double covering, and the designs tend to show a single animal in profile, with rows of zigzags representing bullets (plate 20).[9] The Arapaho often painted a turtle on the shield cover (color, plate 37). Recognizing the difficulty of killing turtles, the Arapaho believed that they themselves would be similarly difficult to kill if they carried the turtle's image. A special type of Cheyenne shield has simple crosshatched lacing taking the place of the heavy rawhide;

needless to say, it would not stop any arrows, but was considered a form of magical protection. Kiowa and Comanche, along with some Pueblo tribes, made their shields by lacing together two layers of rawhide for double thicknesses and, supposedly, for double protection.

The Plains Indians practiced painting their war exploits in a simplified pictographic style. This was a male art, in contrast to the geometric painting done by women. Buffalo robes, tepees, and tepee linings were all often painted with such war chronicles (plates 21–23). Here again stylistic differences between tribes exist, but since this was an individualistic art, the artists in any one tribe might vary more from one another than from artists in neighboring tribes. In general, the older hides show both human and animal figures as "stick figures," with straight lines for limbs, and dashes or hooks for feet and hooves. Later, a more naturalistic style was formed. In general, Northern Plains examples tend to use solidly colored silhouette forms without internal detail while Central Plains examples tend toward simple outline drawings with considerable detail. Some recent examples from the Kiowa have even moved toward the use of perspective and the inclusion of minute detail.

After the reservation areas were set up, and Indians moved to them, much pictographic painting was made in European notebooks and ledgers. These paintings were drawn with trade-colored inks and pencils, but were usually made by Indians for Indian use. However, a commercial development of pictographic painting took place. Paintings on small deer hides or elkskins, and miniature tepee covers were made for sale (color, plate 38). At least one Shoshone man, about 1885, mass-produced painted hides which resembled each other so closely that there is a possibility that they were done with the aid of stencils.[10]

Finally, there is a type of painted object which is common all over the Plains region, the *parfleche*, which is a rawhide container (color, plate 39). It varies from tribe to tribe in details of painting and techniques for lacing. The designs are almost always simple and geometric, being laid out on the flat stretched hide with the aid of willow stick rulers—a method which, of course, determined the geometric character of the pattern. Some tribes will occasionally use curved elements; rarely, a naturalistic design is included on a *parfleche* intended to contain religious equipment (plates 24, 25).[11] Raw or untanned hide was also used for sunshades, rattles, burden straps, and lacing thongs.

The most significant form of sculpture from the Plains takes the form of carved stone pipes (plates 30–33). The usual material is red pipestone (catlinite), found in several localities in Minnesota and Wisconsin. Where this was not available, Indians used shales, soapstones, calcite, chlorite, and limestone. The practice of carving anthropomorphic forms on pipe bowls originated in prehistoric times. In the historic period of the Plains area, the Iowa and

Oto-Missouri produced some of the finest effigy pipes. (The Sioux and Chippewa, living near the Minnesota pipestone quarries, still produce well-carved pipes; though they are for sale to tourists and collectors, they closely resemble those made in the 1830s. A standard modern version has a T-shaped bowl and a carved bison standing on the stem.) Pipe stems carved of green ash wood were also often elaborately decorated, and almost every important visitor to the upper Mississippi River region could be assured of receiving a finely carved and decorated pipe as a ceremonial gift. The stems were usually wrapped with a form of quill plaiting and decorated with woodpecker beaks, mallard duck necks, horsehair, ribbons, and feathers. Some stems lack this added trim, but are decorated with animal forms carved into the wood portion. The Teton Sioux specialize in shallow relief carvings of deer, turtles, sheep, elk, and dragonflies. Santee Sioux and some Woodland groups carve the wood stems into spiral forms.

The typical visual image of the American Indian wearing a flowing feather war bonnet is due in part to the fact that featherwork was an important craft among most of the Plains tribes. The feathers were used in making a variety of head ornaments, but also served as decorations on shields, pipe stems, shirts, leggings, coup sticks, and banners. In addition, feathers were used in a type of dance ornament known as a bustle or "crow belt" (plate 34). Generally, featherwork can be classed as a decorative craft, but some exceptional specimens have considerable aesthetic quality. Some Cheyenne and Arapaho bustles fit this category, with their refined use of cut leather, painted designs, and added trim in the form of bead or quillwork, metal bells, fringes, dyed feathers, and ribbons.

A limited amount of wood carving was done in parts of the Plains area, but was of very minor importance in comparison to the quantity of work produced in the Woodlands. "Love flutes" were often made with carved top blocks; Grass Dance whistles were sometimes carved in bird forms; some bowls were made in the Eastern Plains and various ornaments such as mirror frames and Horse Dance sticks were carved for use in certain dances (plates 40, 41). Some Eastern Plains groups often added carved decoration to their cradle boards. Such boards were a specialty of the Osage and Pawnee, but carving also occurs on some Eastern Sioux boards.

Wooden doll-like fetishes are found in many parts of the Plains. In the Eastern area such types as the Santee Tree Dweller dolls (plate 43) and

7. Beaded pipe bag. Cheyenne. c. 1880. 19″ (less fringe) x 6½″. Denver Art Museum (Cat. No. BS–155). The reverse side of this bag has two hands in place of the two stylized heads. The large beads woven into the fringe are an old Cheyenne–Arapaho characteristic.

8. Beaded pipe bag. Cheyenne. c. 1900. 39 x 6½". Denver Art Museum (Cat. No. BChy–56). Made with small faceted seed beads in the pictographic painting style.

9. Kiowa woman carrying a child in a cradle. Photo by James Mooney in 1893. Note the fully beaded cradle board with overlay beadwork in an abstract floral design. Photo courtesy of the Bureau of American Ethnology, Washington, D.C.

Prairie Potawatomi love dolls were due to an extension of a Woodland tradition. However, dolls are also found in Crow Indian medicine bundles and examples have been noted for the Arapaho. The Eastern Plains area also produced some finely carved wooden war clubs—again probably owing to Woodland influence (plate 44). One type with a wide distribution, but especially favored by the Oto, shows an otter carved in the round, with its head facing the ball of the club. Elk antler was carved much like wood for some specialized uses such as for quirt handles, awl handles, and roach spreaders.

The Plains Indians produced only a limited amount of metalwork, mainly for the decoration of horse headstalls, breast ornaments (plate 45), finger rings, bracelets, earrings, and arm bands.

Other arts practiced on the Eastern Plains as a result of Woodland influence include ribbon appliqué (color, plate 46), loom beadwork, and the making of yarn bags and sashes. Pottery and basketry are extremely rare, and nowhere in the area was true weaving practiced.

10. Lance case, incised buffalo skin, and beads. Crow. Carnegie Museum, Pittsburgh. Fred Harvey Collection (Cat. No. 2418/109)

11. Man's shirt. Mandan (?). c. 1860. Width at shoulders 17″. ⅛Museum of the American Indian, Heye Foundation, New York City (Cat. No. 20/1473). Porcupine quillwork and pony trader beads with designs representing bear paws.

12. Girl's dress. Sioux. c. 1900. Collection Roy H. Robinson, Evanston, Ill. An example of the Sioux tendency to elaborate decoration for the sake of added prestige.

13. Breechclout. Winnebago, Nebraska. 55 x 18″.
State Historical Society of Wisconsin, Madison (Cat.
No. 50.6415). Collected by T. R. Roddy before 1908.
Beaded on list cloth. Although collected from the
Winnebago in Nebraska, it is very unlike Winnebago
work and may have been made by the Oto or a related
tribe.

14. Beaded shirt and leggings on
list cloth. Prairie Potawatomi,
Kansas. c. 1880. Length 51″.
Museum of the American Indian,
Heye Foundation, New York City
(Cat. No. 16/4767)

15. Painted robe. Hidatsa. American Museum of Natural History, New York City (Cat. No. 50.1/6021). A pair of stylized calumet pipes are shown in the center. Note the birdlike designs on the border at top and bottom.

16. Painted shield. Arikara. c. 1850. Diameter 21″. Museum of the American Indian, Heye Foundation, New York City (Cat. No. 15/5624). Collected by M. R. Gilmore on the Fort Berthold reservation in 1915.

17. Cradle board. Crow. c. 1900. 40½ x 11″.
Denver Art Museum (Cat. No. BCr–40)

18. Quiver and bow case. Nez Percé.
c. 1880. Length 60″. Museum of the American
Indian, Heye Foundation, New York City
(Cat. No. 1/4369). Made of otter fur with
bead and red cloth trim.

19. Painted and perforated man's shirt. Blackfeet. c. 1900. Length across sleeves 63". Denver Art Museum (Cat. No. LB 1–1)

20. Painted shield. Crow. c. 1850. Diameter 22". Collection Milford G. Chandler, Detroit. The painting is on a soft buckskin cover which protects a heavy inner rawhide shield.

above: 21. Painted buffalo robe. Tribe unknown.
c. 1830. 62 x 68". Smithsonian Institution, Museum of
Natural History, Washington, D.C. (Cat. No. 2130).
A good example of the older style of simplified
pictographic painting.

right: 22. Painted pictographic buffalo robe. Sioux (?).
Museum für Völkerkunde, Berlin (Cat. No. IVB 208).
Collected by Kohler, 1846.

below: 23. Old Bull's tepee. Sioux. Photo taken by Fiske at
Fort Yates. Photo courtesy of the Bureau of American
Ethnology, Washington, D.C.

24. Incised buffalo rawhide sunshade (detail of front only). Northern Cheyenne. Complete shade 13 x 17″. Collection Richard Pohrt, Flint, Mich. Collected at Fort C. F. Smith in the 1860s. The horses are incised into the leather by scraping away the epidermis.

25. Rawhide cutouts. Oglala Sioux. Man, height 13″; Buffalo, height 8½″. Peabody Museum, Harvard University, Cambridge, Mass. (Cat. Nos. 27498 and 27497). Collected in 1880 by Alice C. Fletcher. These cutouts were suspended from the top of a Sun Dance pole during the annual Sun Dance ceremony.

26. Pony bead cradle.
Comanche. c. 1880. Peabody
Museum, Salem, Mass. (Cat.
No. E38858). Solidly beaded
in gourd stitch.

27. Bandoleer bag. Delaware.
Museum of the American
Indian, Heye Foundation,
New York City (Cat. No.
21/3358). Beaded buckskin
bag with beaded cloth strap.

42

28. Beaded buffalo
robe. Sioux. c. 1870.
71½ x 92″. Denver Art
Museum (Cat. No.
BS–141). Typical
box-and-border design
for a woman's robe, but
unusual for having
beadwork rather than a
painted design.

29. Decorated buffalo
robe. Sioux. c. 1870.
Southwest Museum, Los
Angeles (Cat. No.
630–6–82). A typical
sunburst design done
with porcupine quill
embroidery rather than
with paint.

43

30. Catlinite pipe bowl. Tribe unknown. Peabody Museum, Harvard University, Cambridge, Mass. (Cat. No. 99.12.10/53106). Collected by David Kimball before 1899.

31. Catlinite pipe bowl. Sioux. Length 4⅛″. Smithsonian Institution, Museum of Natural History, Washington, D.C. (Cat. No. 42669). Collected by G. L. Febiger in 1881.

32. Black stone pipe bowl. Cheyenne. Length 10″. Denver Art Museum (Cat. No. PiChy–3)

33. Catlinite pipe bowl. Sioux. Length 10½″. Denver Art Museum (Cat. No. PiS–31). The artist took advantage of the natural variation in the coloring of the stone.

34. Feather bustle. Arapaho. American Museum of Natural History,
New York City (Cat. No. 50/301). Collected by A. L. Kroeber in 1899.
Feather bustles, often called crow belts, are used as an ornament in
the dance. This example is unusual in having a rawhide cutout in the
form of a bird.

35. Painted shield. Sioux. c. 1850. Diameter
20½". Minnesota Historical Society, St. Paul
(Cat. No. E110). Heavy buffalo rawhide
shield with deerskin cover painted in typical
Sioux design.

36. Painted shield. Crow. Carnegie
Museum, Pittsburgh. Fred Harvey
Collection (Cat. No. 2418/116).
Design of a man within a star.

37. Painted shield. Arapaho.
c. 1850. Diameter 19". Museum of
the American Indian, Heye
Foundation, New York City (Cat.
No. 22/8539). Heavy buffalo hide
shield with deerskin cover painted
in a turtle design.

38. Painted buckskin tepee model. Brule Sioux. 39½ x 67". Private collection. Collected by Major L. F. Spencer on the Rosebud reservation in 1888, and probably new at the time of collection.

39. Painted *parfleche*. Cheyenne. c. 1875–1900. 18 x 42". Field Museum of Natural History, Chicago (Cat. No. 97120). This type of *parfleche* is commonly known as a meat case, but it was also used for storing extra clothing and other belongings.

40. Decorated mirror frame. Iowa. 13¼ x 6″. Museum of the American Indian, Heye Foundation, New York City (Cat. No. 14/805). Collected by Milford G. Chandler. Carved of walnut with lead inlay and brass tacks as trim. Such mirrors were carried by dancers in the Grass Dance.

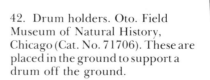

41. Horse Dance sticks. Sioux. Approximate length 35″. Museum of the American Indian, Heye Foundation, New York City (Cat. Nos. 14/1566 and 20/1294). These sticks are carried in a dance to represent a horse ridden into battle.

42. Drum holders. Oto. Field Museum of Natural History, Chicago (Cat. No. 71706). These are placed in the ground to support a drum off the ground.

48

43. Tree Dweller dolls and container. Eastern Sioux. Dolls, heights 6½ and 8⅜"; container, height 10⅜". Colorado State Museum, Denver (Cat. No. 500). Collected by A. D. Osborne in Nebraska before 1908. These dolls are used in an Eastern Sioux variant of the Grand Medicine Lodge ceremonies.

44. Carved wooden war club. Iowa. Length 22¾"; metal blade, length 10". Denver Art Museum (Cat. No. Q1a–1). An otter is carved looking down the blade.

45. Ornament of German silver. Sioux. Width 5⅞". Museum of the American Indian, Heye Foundation, New York City (Cat. No. 12/4437). Ornaments of this type were originally used as frontals on horse bridles and later as chest decorations on Plains Indian men. An eagle design is rocker-engraved on the front.

46. Ribbon appliqué shawl. Osage. 55½ x 67½". Denver Art Museum (Cat. No. AOs–13). A typical example of an Osage woman's blanket on list cloth.

The
Southwest

THE SOUTHWEST

The Southwest area is comprised of the states of New Mexico and Arizona. The land varies considerably from north to south and from east to west. In parts of the area, there are high mountains with piñon pine and juniper blending into arid desert with cactus and sparse vegetation. Its inhabitants comprise three distinct types of culture, with of course the usual variations within each of the three major divisions. The Pueblo peoples have developed a sophisticated agricultural town dwelling society; Navaho and Apache are nomadic hunters; and Papago, Pima, and Yuma had a primitive farming and gathering existence. The land is diverse, the people are diverse, and the culture area is not clearly defined.

The Pueblo farmers live in permanent villages scattered along the Rio Grande in New Mexico, from Taos in the north down to Isleta, just south of Albuquerque; west to Acoma and Laguna and Zuñi; and north to the Hopi villages in Arizona. The Pueblo peoples have occupied the area continuously for well over one thousand years; indeed, some of the present-day villages have been occupied in the same location since before the first Spaniards arrived in 1539. Thanks to the preservative qualities of the dry climate, a good deal is known about the prehistory of the region. The Pueblo peoples are the most conservative and perhaps the most resistant to change of any Indian group in the United States in spite of almost continous and intensive white contact for over four centuries. They were certainly influenced by the early Spanish settlers, but have also managed to retain their aboriginal culture to a surprising degree. Most groups continue to farm with the same primitive tools that their ancestors used, and they continue to plant the same crops of corn, beans, and squash. Corn remains the staple food even though, of course, many villages now have irrigation and a wide variety of newly introduced crops.

Because of their dependence on agriculture in an arid region where agriculture is difficult, the people have developed a complex religious life centered around rainmaking and crop fertility. The rituals are so lengthy that it has been estimated that the average Hopi man spends almost half his time participating in dances or ceremonies. A good deal of energy is spent in making ceremonial clothing and fetishes and learning songs in preparation for the actual performance of the dances. This is men's work, so it is the men in Pueblo villages who make the masks, prayer sticks, and *kachina* dolls.

There are cultural differences between the eastern and western Pueblos, and stylistic differences between every Pueblo, but in general the art of the entire region is very similar. All groups formerly made their own baskets and textiles, and they still make their own pottery. In recent years the Pueblos of Hopi and Zuñi have produced the bulk of the woven textiles such as kilts, belts, sashes, and dresses. Pottery varies from village to village, but as would be expected, neighboring villages often show a blending of styles. Frequently the origin of any piece of painted pottery is determined by a combination of the type of clay used, the thickness of the ware, and the character and color of the design. In general, the style areas for pottery coincide with the geographical proximity of the villages. The Hopi, being somewhat isolated in northeastern Arizona and surrounded by the Navaho reservation, produced a distinctive ceramic ware usually identifiable by the character of the clay. The unslipped ware fires from an orange to a cream in an uneven mottling which is caused by oxidation in firing. Sometimes the pottery is slipped in red, but the orange cream is more common. Designs are painted in red, black, and sometimes white. The forms are usually conventionalizations of natural and human forms (plates 48, 51).

Prehistoric Hopi pottery was much like modern forms, but underwent a slow deterioration until the late nineteenth century. A Tewa potter named Nampeyó from Hano (First Mesa) studied the old pottery and sparked a revival of fine quality ware which has continued to the present. The bulk of what present-day production exists comes from the First Mesa, although it is lacking in both quality and quantity.

The groups to the east of the Hopi—Zuñi, Acoma, Laguna, Santa Ana, Zia, and Isleta—all make a related type of pottery with a white slip and painted designs in red and black. At Zuñi the base part of the pottery is slipped with black or brown in contrast to red or orange at the other villages. In addition, Zuñi pottery is usually decorated with a design laid out in equally divided sections, ranging from two to four. Designs include rosettes and animals with arrows drawn from their mouths to their hearts (plate 2). Since the thinnest pottery in the Southwest is produced at Acoma, this characteristic usually suffices to identify it regardless of its design. The pottery, painted in black and various shades of red orange, tends toward allover patterns of geometric units, or a style, probably borrowed from Zia, of birds and flowers. Some recent floral examples show painting in bright commercial paints after firing. Lucy Lewis, a famous potter from Acoma, has developed a new style based on prehistoric wares in black-on-white. At least three other women at Acoma now produce similar black-on-white wares. It is probable that more pottery is being produced at Acoma today than at any other Pueblo.

At present, the small quantity of pottery produced at Isleta is of a strictly commercial variety.[12] Isleta pottery is often slipped in white all over, including the bottom. A black-on-cream style is common at Santo Domingo, Cochiti, Tesuque, and San Ildefonso. The Santo Domingo ware is very distinctive, with geometric designs being most common (plate 53). A considerable amount of pottery is still being made at Santo Domingo, but mainly for tourist sale. Some of this is in the traditional style, but the bulk of modern production is in black-on-red, red and black-on-cream, or a polished red ware with polychrome painting after firing. Much of this recent pottery is decorated with floral designs. Cochiti, San Felipe, and Tesuque tend toward small designs on a basically cream background. Some potters at Cochiti used to make a quantity of realistic human and animal forms for tourist sale, but these are uncommon today. Very little old style Tesuque pottery is available. The most common forms from this Pueblo now are the small so-called "rain gods" produced for tourist sale, and poorly fired red ware painted with bright poster paints after firing.

Although the black-on-cream ware was common at San Ildefonso during the last century, this Pueblo is most noted for the polished black-on-black invented by Maria and Julian Martinez about 1919. These pots are painted after polishing, so that the painted area appears as dull black on a polished black surface. The painting is done by men after the women have made the basic ware, an unusual departure from the common practice where women make the pots from start to finish. About 1931, still another type of ware in the form of designs carved into the pot in low relief was introduced at San Ildefonso by Rosalie Aguilar. The Pueblo of Santa Clara, being situated right next to San Ildefonso, makes a very similar pottery type. Santa Clara produces the standard polished red or polished black varieties as well as the black-on-black and carved forms. Some of the pottery made at San Juan is also of the polished red or black variety; however, San Juan's specialty is pottery which is partially slipped and polished on the top rim only. San Juan also has a revival of a prehistoric form which consists of a light brown ware with fine scratched lines, usually in geometric designs.

Still another distinct pottery type is produced at Taos and Picuris Pueblos in the northern part of the Southwest area. Here the clay has a high mica content. The pottery is unslipped to produce a brownish ware which has a glistening surface owing to reflections from the mica.

In addition to work in all these basic traditional forms, there has been a considerable amount of experimentation with new clays, new shapes, and new decorative techniques at various Pueblos. The incentive usually stems from an effort to produce more salable wares to non-Indians. Both San Ildefonso and Santa Clara have developed a finely painted polychrome ware that has had mild commercial success. But in general, pottery is a dying art. At any one Pueblo only a few women still make it, and of course, in some Pueblos no pottery is made at all.

Basketry is practiced in many of the Pueblos, but is usually very simple, undecorated work. Plaited yucca leaves were used for mats and winnowing trays at several villages, but these items are only made at Jemez and in the

Hopi towns today. The finest baskets are made by the Hopi in two different techniques. On the Third Mesa the women specialize in wicker baskets made on frameworks of sumac. These take the form of round trays with colorful designs worked into them (plate 54). The patterns, done in native dyes, usually represent *kachinas*, while birds and whirlwind patterns are also common. On the Second Mesa the specialty is a type of coiled basket made of yucca leaves around a grass core (plate 55). While the technique is completely different, the designs and colors are very similar to those used on the Third Mesa.

Weaving is an old Pueblo craft. In early times the principal material, a type of native cotton, was grown to be spun. Of course, after the introduction of sheep by the Spanish, wool was commonly used for decoration, often as embroidery on a cotton garment (plate 57; color, plates 49, 50). Throughout the Pueblo area, weaving was man's work. Kilts, belts, and sashes had to be woven for use in ceremonial dances. Among the Hopi, men also made the wedding costume for their brides. The woven designs, mainly consisting of transverse stripes, are usually quite simple; however, the construction itself is often rather elaborate. Although a plain basket-weave was common, Pueblo weavers were able to produce complex twills in diamond and herringbone patterns. Men's sashes were made in a type of brocade called "false embroidery," and women's belts were ornamented by a system of floating the warps to produce a design. A special type of white belt, known as a "rain sash," is done by braiding, the strands becoming alternately both warp and weft. The most elaborate garments are those with true embroidery which is often in complex, colorful designs. Except in the Hopi villages, the women do all the embroidery.

The Hopi are the principal producers of woven materials, the center being the villages of Hotevila and Shimopovi, and while other Pueblo groups occasionally make floated-warp belts, embroider commercial cotton cloth, or knit or crochet stockings and leggings, most of their ceremonial clothing is obtained in trade from Hopi weavers.

The items made in connection with the religious ritual are often some of the most impressive products of the Pueblo craftsman. The *kachinas*, or godlike spirits, always make their appearance in the dances wearing characteristic masks, some of which are extremely elaborate in form. Masked ritual was most highly developed in the western Pueblos, and especially at Hopi and Zuñi. Little is known about *kachina* ritual at some of the northern Rio Grande Pueblos, and it is believed to be absent altogether from Taos and Picuris. The Hopi and Zuñi often allow non-Indians to witness masked dances. The other Pueblos prohibit spectators altogether.

The masks are usually made of heavy leather or rawhide in a variety of basic shapes (plates 58, 60, 61). Some cover only the face; others, inverted cylinders in form, cover the entire head. These masks are repainted with appropriate designs before each dance, and appendages such as ears, mouth, and nose are made from feathers and fur (or evergreen) ruffs. Often the same basic mask can be used to represent several different *kachinas* by a change of ornaments and painted designs. In former years these masks, along with other ceremonial equipment, were jealously guarded in the *kivas*, and only a few were collected before the turn of the century. Now a few which have never been ceremonially used are being made strictly for sale. This breakdown in religious restrictions is a result of several factors. Some of the material is being offered for sale by Indians living off the reservations, but a good deal of it becomes available due to marriages between tribes. For example, a Zuñi man married to a Laguna woman and living at Zuñi might still observe the taboos against selling religious equipment, but his wife would not be under the same obligations.

At Hopi, Zuñi, Acoma, Jemez, and Laguna, the people make small wooden dolls carved to represent *kachinas* (plates 62, 63, 65). These are given to the young girls to play with, and also so that the children can learn about their religion. The Hopi are the principal producers of *kachina* dolls, which are a fairly recent innovation in that the oldest example known dates from about 1879. Old dolls are quite flat with little detail of hands or feet. This style has continued to the present in a type of doll given to infants. However, there has been a tendency toward realism and natural bodily proportions, with even muscles depicted. The material most often used today is the soft root wood of the cottonwood tree.

Zuñi dolls can often be distinguished from Hopi ones by two signs: the Zuñi dolls' arms are frequently movable at the shoulders, and they are dressed in actual cloth apparel rather than painted clothing. The limited number of dolls known from Jemez, Acoma, and Laguna resemble the older Hopi forms without any indications of legs or arms. Hopi dolls are fairly common in collections; in fact, the Hopi have developed a considerable market for dolls. Until recently, dolls from Zuñi were quite scarce and Acoma and Laguna dolls were almost unknown. Now these three groups are also following the Hopi pattern of making dolls for sale.

Stone or wood fetishes are carved for a variety of religious usages by most Pueblo groups. Often they are used as shrine figures or offerings in the *kivas* (sacred underground chambers), or in holy places that are situated away from the village proper. The wooden war gods made at Zuñi are well known (plate 68); new ones are still made each year. Equally impressive are the war god images of Acoma and Laguna, and the wooden shrine figures carved for altars in Hopi and Zuñi *kivas*. The animal fetishes made of hard stone probably represent the highest development of stone carving among Indians in historic times (color, plate 4). These fetishes are excelled only by some of the stone carvings produced in the Northwest Coast area. Unfortunately, because of the tremendous demand for these stone fetishes among collectors, they have been faked in large numbers. It is often difficult to distinguish the authentic from the spurious.

Stone and shell were commonly used for jewelry. Turquoise was locally mined, and prized for its decorative value everywhere among the Pueblo people. Shells, on the other hand, had to be imported from Mexico or California. Because they were rare and were associated with water, they also were valued ornaments. Some silver jewelry was probably made by Pueblo smiths from the latter part of the nineteenth century onward, but it so much resembles Navaho work that it is not usually recognized as being of Pueblo manufacture. Within the last thirty years, however, the Hopi have developed a rather distinctive style utilizing cutout silver soldered over sheet silver with the recessed portion of the design being blackened with "liver of sulphur" (impure potassium sulfide). These Hopi designs are derived from pottery decoration, and have a very contemporary appearance. The silver industry at Zuñi has flourished in recent years, with as many women smiths as men. The work is often characterized by the use of many small turquoise sets, or by elaborate inlays of blue turquoise, black jet, and red spiny oyster shell. The smiths at Santo Domingo produce a wide variety of ornaments, most of which are very like the Navahos' work; only a few special Santo Domingo types have been developed, such as brooches utilizing animal forms. In general, Santo Domingo work is produced for sale, and is made of thin silver and set with turquoise of poor quality; however, some designs made for local use are as good as the best made anywhere in the area.

Painting has always been a Pueblo art, since prehistoric times when artists worked on pottery and *kiva* walls. In addition, some groups such as the Hopi made dry sand paintings for some *kiva* ceremonies, simple naive designs on pottery tiles, and elaborate designs on Butterfly Dance *tablitas*. Shortly after 1900, the American anthropologist Jesse Walter Fewkes encouraged two Hopi artists to produce a series of watercolor sketches of *kachina* figures for a study he was making on Hopi religion. They were followed by other Indian artists who produced paintings on paper for sale to tourists. By 1917 this tendency was fully developed at San Ildefonso where several artists were devoting much of their time to painting. Art classes were taught in the Indian schools in Santa Fé and also in Oklahoma, and art was generally encouraged. Today there are well over one hundred artists from the Plains, Navaho, and Apache, who are every bit as good as the Pueblo artists (color, plates 56, 59, 64). Everywhere the style is characterized by use of watercolors or caseins in a flat outline painting. Bright colors are the rule and no effort is made at shading, but minute detail is shown in very fine lines. Today this art is very much alive, and several annual competitive exhibits are held at the Philbrook Art Center in Tulsa, the Gallup Intertribal Indian Ceremonial, at the Museum of New Mexico, at Scottsdale, Arizona, and elsewhere. Most present-day artists continue to paint in the fine-line flat style; however, a few are experimenting with new techniques and styles and are producing some exciting work.

The Pueblo peoples have, in general, resisted change with vigor. It sometimes seems that they firmly believe their way of living is the best possible, and that if their ceremonies were ever to stop, the world might come to an end. But in spite of the tenacity with which they cling to their old culture, many influences have affected them, and in a number of fields a good deal of change has occurred. Since these people have been in contact with Spanish settlers for some four hundred years, for instance, they have inevitably adopted some Spanish elements into their culture. All Pueblo villages have a Catholic church, and the people are devout Catholics although they maintain their own religions as well. If having one religion is good, they feel, then having two is better. Many Pueblo men speak at least three languages, their own tribal language, English, and Spanish. Sometimes they can add a little Navaho, or the language of a neighboring village as well. It has been said that by watching a Pueblo man change his clothing you can see the influences of three cultures. His undergarment is often still the native breechclout, but now made of commercial cotton cloth. Over this he will wear a pair of trousers cut in the Spanish style with flaring bottoms and a slit up the outside. And over this goes a pair of commercially manufactured pants.

The northern Rio Grande groups have also received considerable influence from the Plains tribes (colorplates 66, 67). At Taos, the men and women formerly wore leather shirts and dresses, and the men still wear a Plains type hard-sole moccasin. However, perhaps the most obvious cultural exchange has been in Hopi influences on the Navaho.

47. Pair of batons for Marau ceremony. Hopi. 20⅞ x 4¾". Denver Art Museum (Cat. Nos. QH–55 and 56)

48. Pottery bowl. Hopi. Diameter 9¾". Denver Art Museum (Cat No. XH–5). A shallow bowl with a painting representing the Polik Mana or Butterfly Maiden.

49. Embroidered manta. Hopi. 48½ x 80". Denver Art Museum (Cat. No. RHc–92)

50. Woman's dress. Acoma Pueblo. c. 1875. 46 x 56″. American Museum of Natural History, New York City. Embroidered on wool.

51. Painted pottery tiles. Hopi. Maximum size 6½ x 4¼″. Denver Art Museum. These show the simple childlike painting style common in the Pueblo area during the later part of the nineteenth century.

52. Pottery bowl. Zia. Diameter
13½″. Denver Art Museum (Cat.
No. XZ–26–G). A modern bowl
form, but with a typical Zia-style
bird design.

53. Pottery jar. Santo Domingo
Pueblo. Height 9¾″. Denver Art
Museum (Cat. No. XSD–90)

54. Wicker basketry trays. Hopi from Third Mesa. Diameters 13 to 15″. Denver Art Museum (Cat. Nos. YH3–19, 51, and 52)

55. Coiled basketry trays. Hopi from Second Mesa. Diameters 13 to 14″. Denver Art Museum (Cat. Nos. XH2–9, 8, and 32)

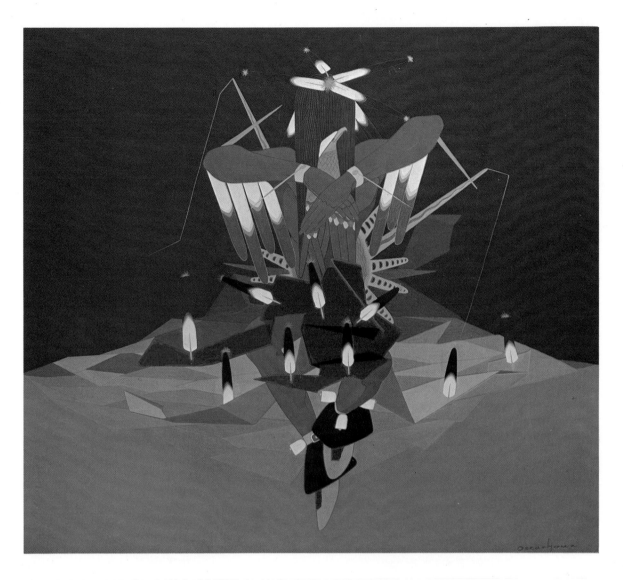

56. *Sioux Dancer*. Watercolor. Denver Art Museum (Cat. No. PS–26).
Painted by Oscar Howe, a Sioux artist.

57. Embroidered shirt. Jemez
Pueblo. Center panel 19½ x
23″. Denver Art Museum
(Cat. No. RJ–3). Collected at
Jemez in 1916.

58. *Kachina* mask.
Laguna Pueblo. Height
8¾". Denver Art
Museum (Cat. No.
NL–2)

59. *Navaho Shepherds
at Waterhole.* Casein.
Denver Art Museum
(Cat. No. PN–16).
Painted by Harrison
Begay, a Navaho artist.

60. *Kachina* mask. From the Tewa village of Hano. Height 8¾". University Museum, Philadelphia (Cat. No. 38720). The mask is of leather with cloth ball eyes and carved wooden protruding teeth.

61. *Kachina* mask. Zuñi Pueblo. Height 9". Brooklyn Museum, New York (Cat. No. 04.187). Represents Anahoho, one of the gods of the Salimopia.

62. *Kachina* doll. Hopi. Height 6⅝". Denver
Art Museum (Cat. No. QH–153). Collected
by James Stevenson on First Mesa in the
winter of 1885–86. Represents Pawik
kachina.

63. *Kachina* doll. Zuñi. Height
21⅝". Denver Art Museum (Cat.
No. QZu–33). Shows mudheads
climbing a pole.

64. *Herding Sheep.* Watercolor. Denver Art Museum (Cat. No. PAC–3). Painted by Allan Houser, an Apache artist.

65. Warrior *kachina* doll. Hopi. 1954. Height 16¼″. Denver Art Museum (Cat. No. QH–195). An example of the trend toward realism in commercial dolls.

68

66. Painted and beaded
elkskin robe. Taos Pueblo.
48 x 60″. Denver Art
Museum (Cat. No. PTa–1).
Although made at Taos
Pueblo for local use, the
actual maker was a Ute.

67. Shield. Tesuque Pueblo.
c. 1850. Diameter 20″.
Southwest Museum, Los
Angeles (Cat. No. 491 G 1058)

69

68. War god figure. Zuñi Pueblo.
Height 27½". Denver Art Museum
(Cat. No. QZu–44). Collected by
Arthur G. Clark about 1900.

69. Butterfly Dance *tablita*. Hopi
Pueblo. 19½ x 11½". Denver Art
Museum (Cat. No. QH–7)

70

The Southern Athabascans

The Navaho and Apache groups both speak related languages of the Athabascan linguistic family, but they are quite different in their way of living. Most of the Athabascan-speaking peoples are situated in the far north of interior Canada and Alaska. Thus it is generally believed that these two groups migrated from the North at some date before the historic period.

The Navaho are today the largest tribe in the United States, and own the largest reservation. They number over seventy-five thousand people, with little racial admixture, living in scattered family units over parts of Arizona, New Mexico, and Utah. Formerly the Navaho were semi-nomadic, practicing some agricultural techniques learned from the Pueblo people, but also hunting small game and utilizing a variety of natural vegetable foods. They were generally quite warlike and often raided the Pueblo villages for their crops when they were ripe, or the Spanish settlements for horses and other booty. After the introduction of domestic animals, the Navaho became sheep herders; at present, many families depend upon sheep as their main source of food, supplemented by packaged foodstuffs purchased at a local trading post.

The Navaho have preferred to live in close proximity to their Pueblo neighbors and have borrowed many cultural elements from Hopi and Zuñi. The famous dry sand paintings, made by the Navaho as part of several important healing ceremonies, are an art form which was probably derived from a simpler Hopi style. However, the Navaho have a tendency, even when borrowing, to elaborate and adapt other forms to their own cultural styles so that the final product is always distinctly Navaho in feeling. This is equally true of their textiles. The techniques were borrowed from the Pueblos, but the finished work was often more elaborate than—and far superior to—the simpler Pueblo work.

Sand paintings are made on dry sand with natural earth colors, ground shell, charcoal, and pollen. They are usually completed in one day and then destroyed in the ritual process of transferring the magic potency of the painting to the patient being cured. Several efforts have been made to preserve these paintings either in the form of watercolors, by weaving the sand painting designs into rugs (plate 71), or by various techniques of glueing the sand on a board backing. The older religious taboo against making a complete sand painting for commercial use has weakened, due to a combination of a breakdown in the religion and a desire for monetary gain. This has gone so far that in recent years a popular craft form involves using the paintings

71

preserved on boards as framed pictures, or even setting these paintings in tabletops.

The Navaho learned weaving some two hundred sixty years ago from the Hopi and Zuñi, and the styles of textiles have changed continually since then. At first the Navaho copied the simple banded designs used by their Pueblo neighbors when they wove blankets or dresses for the women. Later, designs became more complex and better yarns were introduced. A host of local styles developed; later still, revivals of some older forms were urged by the traders. The historical sequence shows first the use of hand-spun wool and native dyes. This was followed by the use of raveled commercial cloth from English stroud, in red ("bayeta") and blue, and some raveled green blanket yarn, and then the introduction of commercially spun wool (called "Germantown" or "Saxony"), and brightly hued aniline dyes (color, plate 76). Recent weavers have revived the use of native dyes, and a new type of blanket, the border blanket, developed at the trading posts of Crystal and Two Grey Hills (plate 72). The lightweight clothing blankets became heavy rugs as production turned from Indian use to manufacture for sale to tourists. Today this industry is still very much alive—each reservation area produces distinct local styles—but it is not economically sound. Increasingly, Navaho women are turning from weaving blankets to more profitable work. Probably the complete disappearance of Navaho weaving is not too distant.

Silver ornaments are still made in large quantity (plate 73). About 1853, the Navaho evidently learned from the Mexicans, how to work silver, but did not do so in any quantity until about 1870. Navaho smiths borrowed designs from both Mexican and Plains Indian sources, but—as with sand painting and weaving—adapted the designs into forms which are distinctly their own. They soon excelled their instructors in quality. Early work was made from silver coins either hammered into sheets or melted in molds, and later replaced with sheet or ingot silver supplied by the traders. Generally, Navaho work is fairly heavy and often set with large turquoise stones.

The Navaho also make a very simple type of pottery in small quantity. Decorated ware was once made, but now only a limited number of crude cooking pots are to be found. These forms are sometimes converted into drums by the addition of skin tympani over the openings. Baskets were formerly made by Navahos, and some are still used in certain ceremonies. These, however, are generally made for the Navaho by their neighbors the Apache, Ute, and Paiute. A very limited use of masks is found in at least one Navaho healing rite—the Yei-be-chai Dance (plates 74, 75). These masks were probably also inspired by Pueblo prototypes.

It should be pointed out that "Apache" is a general term for several related tribes which once roamed over much of southern and central Arizona, eastern New Mexico, and parts of west Texas. Each of these bands developed distinct characteristics; nevertheless, they are all closely related. In their beaded leather garments, the Jicarilla in northern New Mexico closely resemble Plains tribes, especially the Ute. To a lesser extent the Mescalero and Lipan also show some Plains traits; the San Carlos and Fort Apache groups (the principal basket producers) show less Plains influence.

The Apache in the Southwest are much like the Navaho in social organization, religion, and mythology, but lack the Pueblo influences. They produce no textiles, no sand paintings, and very little silverwork. Instead, they, and especially the Western Apache groups, have excelled in basketry (plate 77).

The Apache attach the same importance to healing ceremonies as the Navaho, but their one major religious celebration is a puberty ceremony for girls. Its public dance portion is usally known as the Mountain Spirit Dance (sometimes erroneously called the "Devil Dance") in which the male dancers wear spectacular tall slat crowns above cloth or leather hoods (plates 80, 81).

70. Group of Navaho weavers. The woman on the left is spinning yarn, the small girl is carding. The loom on the right is for weaving a floated warp belt. Photo courtesy of the Bureau of American Ethnology, Washington, D.C.

71. Sand painting type rug.
Navaho. 66 x 64″. Denver Art
Museum (Cat. No. RN–96). A copy
in weaving of a design used in the
Male Shooting Chant ceremony.

72. Two Grey Hills rug. Navaho.
1948. 70½ x 49¾″. Denver Art
Museum (Cat. No. RN–86). Woven
by Daisy Touglechee near
Toadlena, New Mexico. This is an
extremely fine piece of weaving,
with ninety wefts to the inch and
made with handspun yarn.

74

73. Silverwork. Navaho. Smithsonian Institution, Museum of Natural History, Washington, D.C. Early examples of conchas and buckles.

74. Mask. Navaho. Brooklyn Museum, New York (Cat. No. 03.184). For use in the Yei-be-chai Dance.

75. Mask. Navaho. Brooklyn Museum, New York (Cat. No. 03.183)

76. Germantown yarn rug. Navaho.
c. 1885–90. 29½ x 54½". Denver
Art Museum (Cat. No. RNsd–36)

77. Large storage basket. Western
Apache. Diameter 12¾". Denver
Art Museum (Cat. No. YA–124)

76

78. Rawhide playing cards. Apache.
3½ x 2¼". Museum of the
American Indian, Heye
Foundation, New York City (Cat.
No. 6/4597). Made by Indians in
imitation of Spanish playing cards.

79. Painted deerskin. Chiricahua
Apache. 33 x 51". Museum of the
American Indian, Heye
Foundation, New York City (Cat.
No. 20/3519)

80. Apache Crown or Mountain Spirit Dancers. From a photo taken before 1900. Photo courtesy of the American Bureau of Ethnology, Washington, D.C.

81. Crown Dance headdresses. White River Apache. American Museum of Natural History, New York City

82. Painted bag and fetish. White Mountain Apache. Bag, 9½ x 3½". Denver Art Museum (Cat. Nos. PA–1 and QA–18). Collected in 1903 by C. L. Owen.

78

The Rancheria Tribes

The Pima, Papago, and Yuman—collectively the Rancheria tribes—form still a third major subdivision of the Southwest area, in southwestern Arizona, and along the Colorado and Gila rivers. It is generally believed that the Pima and Papago, two closely related tribes, are the descendants of the prehistoric Hohokam of the region. These people practiced some agriculture, but depended to a considerable extent upon mesquite, cactus, and fish for food. These tribes show a limited amount of Pueblo influences, and probably served as a link between the Pueblo and southern California tribes. It is surprising, however, that the Pueblo groups did not influence a wider area. A few groups practiced simple weaving of cotton textiles, but this craft has been extinct for at least one hundred years. Pima and Papago had traces of Pueblo ritual practices in their ceremonies to bring rain and crop fertility, including some masked dances. Pima also had developed a form of crop irrigation, and the southwestern Arizona area is one of the few parts of the country where fermented beverages were produced.

Pima and Papago groups excelled in basketry, using a coiled technique. They used these baskets in trade with their Yuman neighbors. Some pottery was produced throughout this area as far as southern California, but it was generally quite crude and poorly fired. The Mohave and their neighbors along the Colorado River, the Yuma, Maricopa, and Cocopa produced painted pottery dolls and vessels with pottery heads. Some of these, while crude, have a certain strength of effect (plates 84–86; color, plate 83).

With the exception of basketry, the arts were generally poorly developed in the entire Rancheria region. The Yuman groups practiced some beadwork in a netted technique; certain examples done in only blue and white beads strikingly resemble elaborate basketry designs. The Yuman Havasupai and Walapai living in the Grand Canyon area of northwestern Arizona produced a limited amount of basketry, but little else. The Papago still produce baskets in quantity and, surprisingly, their quality has improved in recent years.

The Pima and Maricopa still make a limited amount of pottery of a polished red or cream decorated with black paint. The Mohave and Colorado River tribes still occasionally produce pottery in an unpolished buff and brown. Pottery is certainly a dying art in the area, but Papago basketry will probably survive for at least a couple of generations.

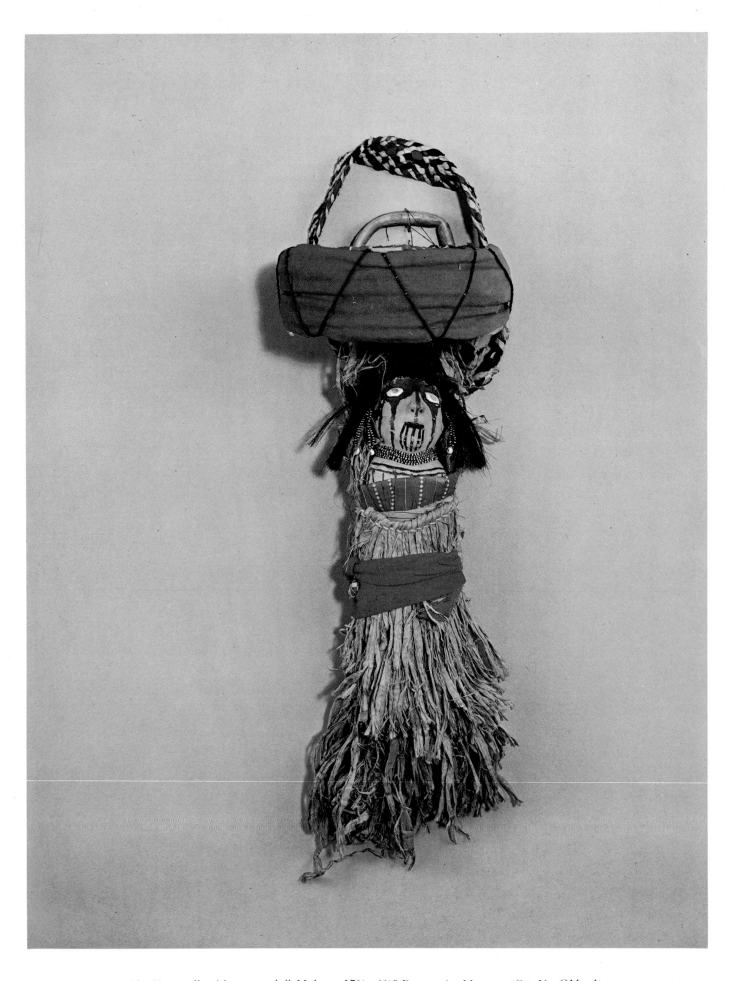

83. Toy cradle with pottery doll. Mohave. 17¾ x 4¾″. Denver Art Museum (Cat. No. QMo–1)

84. Clay doll. Mohave. Peabody Museum, Harvard University, Cambridge, Mass. (Cat. No. 72.26.10/7062). Collected by Jules Marcon in 1854.

85. Pottery figure. Cocopa. Peabody Museum, Harvard University, Cambridge, Mass. (Cat. No. 84105)

86. Pottery doll. Mohave. Height
8⅞″. Denver Art Museum (Cat. No.
TMo–4)

California

The Great Basin
and the Pacific Plateau

The Pacific Northwest Coast

CALIFORNIA

Almost all the state of California is generally considered an independent area. The Sierra Nevada and the desert to the east formed an effective barrier to east–west cultural exchanges, so that the California Indians were fairly isolated from the outside. The southern part of the state shows only some influence from the Southwest sand paintings and pottery, while the northern part reveals some from the Northwest Coast area in the use of wooden houses and carved spirit figures.

The entire area was densely populated in precontact times by many small and scattered tribes belonging to several linguistic families. Throughout the state, living was fairly easy, food abundant, and the climate mild. The people practiced no agriculture, but depended on food gathering. The acorn was the staff of life throughout most of California, supplemented by wild plants, seafood, and the catch from hunting. Clothing was scanty, even non-existent in some areas. Everywhere the level of technology was very primitive, with the major exception of basketry: California Indians produced some of the finest baskets in the world. Weaving was unknown, but a type of knot netting was produced with native fibers. Feathers were often used for decoration on baskets, hair pins, belts, headdresses, and even on capes.

The degree of white contact was, at first, inconsistent. Spanish missions and settlements were created quite early along the coast from San Diego to San Francisco, and many of the neighboring coastal groups became extinct at an early date. Other northern and interior tribes received almost no white contact until the 1849 Gold Rush, and were able to maintain their aboriginal way of life to a late date. As recently as 1911 an Indian was found who had had no contact with whites, and who was still making stone arrowpoints.[13]

From the standpoint of technology and style, the state is often divided into three areas, from south to north. The small groups who used to live in southern California are collectively known as Mission Indians (they early settled around the Spanish missions) or by the derogatory name "diggers," after their use of wild plant roots for food. Many of these groups are now extinct owing to white pressures and to diseases; those still existing retain very few vestiges of their former culture. Previously, however, they manufactured a finely made type of coiled basket in rich red brown tones and, often, naturalistic rattlesnake designs. Besides these, they produced some poorly made pottery in an unslipped, usually unpainted, red ware. Stone carvings—sandstone bowls and soapstone figures—were common; some

85

soapstone animal effigies with inset shell beads are beautifully proportioned and naturalistic. Most were probably made before white contact.

Influences from the Southwest can be seen in the pottery (scanty as it is), the use of boomerang-like rabbit sticks, sandals, and especially the sand paintings made for the puberty ceremonies of boys. These paintings are usually quite simple even in comparison to Hopi paintings. The ceremonies involve the use of the so-called "Jimson weed" (*Datura stramonium*), a dangerous narcotic.

In the central California area, which is considered typical for the state, no pottery is produced and little woodwork, although basketry is highly developed. Both the coiled technique of the southern area and the twined techniques of the north are utilized in a variety of basketry types. Here the baskets are not only technically excellent, but the designs and forms are elegant in their simplicity. The Pomo tribe is especially well known for baskets ranging in size from three feet in diameter to those smaller than a pea. The so-called "jewel" or "gift" baskets, covered with brightly colored natural feathers and shell pendants, are a specialty of this tribe (colorplate 93).

In the northern part of the state, some influences drifted down from the Northwest Coast area. Some northern California groups made plank houses and dugout canoes. They used rod-and-slat armor and wore basketry hats. The baskets were as fine as those produced in the central area. Yurok and Karok, in particular, made beautifully shaped baskets with knobbed lids, often decorated with yellow porcupine quills and the natural rich brown of the maidenhair fern stem (plate 88).

A specifically Northern trait is the use of elk antler for spoons which, with carved designs on the delicate handles, must have been extremely difficult to manufacture with primitive tools. The actual techniques have long been forgotten (plate 89).

With the exception of the prehistoric soapstone carvings, a limited amount of featherwork (plate 90), a few fine elk antler carvings, and a very few wood carvings from the northern area (plate 91), the entire California area is mainly notable for its basketry. In general the baskets are technically excellent. The colors are the natural plant browns and blacks; the design elements are often simple geometric units of squares, triangles, diamonds, and zigzags. Exceptions are the naturalistic designs on Mission baskets, the yellow porcupine quills on Karok baskets, and the feathers used by the Pomo. Anyone examining a large collection of baskets from the entire state cannot help but be impressed by the tremendous variety of sizes and shapes, as well as by the vast number of plants utilized.

At the turn of the century, several women were still producing baskets of high quality. Some achieved a limited degree of fame for the excellence of their work. The Pomo woman Mary Benson and Dat-so-la-lee, a Washo, produced baskets which were eagerly sought by collectors (plate 92).

Today the art of basketry is almost extinct, except that occasionally a very few women weave a basket for sale. Religion survives to some extent. Ceremonies are still performed, with the participants wearing costumes which are heirlooms among the Hupa and Yurok of northern California.

87. Coiled basket. Tulare. Height 8½". Denver Art Museum (Cat. No. YTu–18). The feathers are the top-knots from the California quail.

88. Twined basket with lid. Karok. Height with lid 6¾". Denver Art Museum (Cat. No. YKa–58). Collected by Grace Nicholson.

89. Elk antler spoons. Karok, Yurok, and Hupa. Longest spoon 6¾". Denver Art Museum (Cat. Nos. QKa–19; QKa–17; QYu–21; QKa–18; QHu–7)

90. Pair of woman's feathered ear plugs. Pomo. Length 7¼". Denver Art Museum (Cat. No. FPo–12). Made of an engraved crane wing bone, with feather-covered basketry disc and shell pendants.

91. Wooden effigy of Pock-San-e (place in meadow) Chuck-e-yok (big boy). Klamath. Peabody Museum, Harvard University, Cambridge, Mass. Gift of Lewis H. Farlow (Cat. No. 10.21.10/76535). Collected by Grace Nicholson and Mr. Hartman in 1910. The placement of the arms coming out from the chest is an unusual treatment.

92. Basket bowl. Washo. Diameter 10″. University Museum, Philadelphia (Cat. No. 38–26–1). Made by the famous Washo basket maker, Dat-so-la-lee.

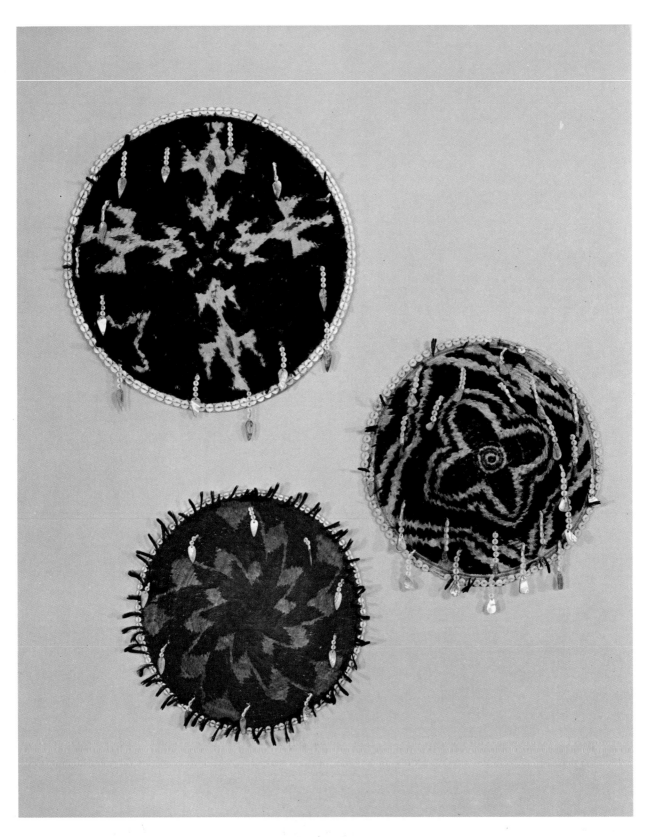

93. Three feather baskets. Pomo. Diameter of largest basket 13½".
Denver Art Museum (Cat. Nos. YPo–145, 154, and 157)

THE GREAT BASIN AND THE PACIFIC PLATEAU

The Great Basin and Pacific Plateau groups are often included with those of California in a single great "intermountain" culture area; but although there are many similarities between all of these areas, on a stylistic basis it is preferable to discuss the Basin and Plateau arts as distinct entities. The Great Basin comprises the area between the Rocky Mountains on the east and the Sierra Nevada on the west, the largely barren deserts of Utah, Nevada, and southern Oregon. The scattered bands of Paiute and Shoshone Indians living in this region are the most primitive of any in the United States. They, like their California neighbors, were often called diggers. Theirs is a bare subsistence economy based on seed gathering, supplemented by a little hunting of small game. They utilize almost all the potential food products of their environment, including even insects and grubs. Food gathering consumes almost all their waking hours, allowing little time for artistic production. The Basin groups live in very simple brush shelters. They produce little pottery, and only a limited amount of crude basketry. Some Washo groups, along the California–Nevada border, produced finely made basketry, but the usual baskets were the pitch-covered water jars, or the coiled plaques, often traded to the Navaho in the south. Their only form of weaving was a type of blanket woven from strips of rabbit fur.

Some Basin groups still produce a limited number of tanned hides, beaded novelties, and some basketry. Baskets or commercial glass bottles completely covered with beadwork were latterly a Paiute specialty, and a few are still made even now. The Washo, Paiute, and Shoshone on the Pyramid Lake reservation at Dixon, Nevada, have formed an arts and crafts cooperative known as Wa-Pai-Shone Craftsmen. The Ghost Dance religion, launched about 1889 by Wovoka, a Paiute prophet from the Pyramid Lake reservation, had little effect on the arts of the Basin area; on the other hand, it introduced a new art form to many Plains tribes. The prophet foretold that if the Indians performed the new dance, refrained from fighting, and did no harm to anyone but always did what was right, then the buffalo would return, the white man would disappear, and all the dead would return to life. The Sioux, Cheyenne, Kiowa, and Arapaho all developed specially painted shirts, to be worn during the dances, which the faithful thought possessed the magical property of invulnerability to bullets (plate 94).

The Plateau area is composed of portions of Idaho and Washington to the east of the coast range, inland British Columbia, and northern Oregon. The area is somewhat less isolated than the Great Basin because travel is feasible on the Columbia and Fraser rivers. The people here subsisted largely on roots and berries, but also depended heavily upon the salmon and other fish from the rivers. There are many tribes in this area belonging mainly to the Salishan and Sahaptian linguistic families. They formerly lived in semi-subterranean houses or in mat-covered lodges, but in later years adopted the Plains type of tepee covered either with skin or bulrush mats.

Throughout all this area basketry was developed to a fine art in both coiled and twined techniques. Twining was used mainly for soft bags and hats, and coiling for large storage containers. Coiled baskets from this area often have a distinctive form of decoration known as "imbrication" which consists of sewing decorative elements on the outer surface of the baskets made with the regular coiled stitches (plate 95). Imbricated baskets are often assigned to the Klickitat tribe, but were also made by Yakima, Lillooet, Shuswap, Chilcotin, Thompson, and Fraser Indians. The Nez Percé produced a distinctive type of flat twined wallet with polychrome designs worked in with a false embroidery (plate 96). Here again, however, although the Nez Percé were the principal makers of such basket wallets, they were also made by their neighbors, the Umatilla and Walla Walla. These people made no pottery, but did have dugout canoes for river travel.

The Plateau peoples show a considerable number of Plains traits, although when and how these influences made themselves felt is not clear. They developed a horse culture to a high degree, and the Cayuse and Nez Percé tribes were noted for their breeding of the appaloosa. Horse trappings in the form of saddles, martingales, and cruppers were very similar in style to those made by the Crow in the Plains themselves (plate 97). Likewise, the costumes of both men and women were made of skin in Crow style, although some recent examples seem to show more influence from the Blackfeet. Since the turn of the century, the beadwork of the Plateau groups, as with those of the Northern Plains, seems to have changed from the use of geometric to floral motifs. In the inland area of British Columbia, several influences from the Northwest Coast area can be traced. The Lillooet and Thompson peoples made carved figures used as grave monuments representing totems, simple carved stone bowls, and crude blankets of dog hair and mountain goat wool (color, plate 107). Some groups, like the Shuswap, produced birchbark baskets resembling those from the Great Lakes area.

The upper Chinook groups, Wishram and Wasco, living along the Columbia River near The Dalles, Oregon, developed a quite distinct style usually referred to as "X-ray" owing to the fact that ribs, for instance, are shown as if exposed. Baskets in flat or pail-like form are twined, with human and animal figures showing this X-ray character (plate 98). Figures of the same type are carved on bowls and spoons of sheep horn as well as of wood;

they can sometimes also be found on wooden mortars and antler adze handles (plates 99–105). These Wishram and Wasco groups are now scattered and intermingled with other Indians on the Yakima reservation in Washington and the Warm Springs reservation in Oregon. Early reports indicate that these people at one time had a rich decorative art, but few examples are known today.[14] The sketch of a canoe prow carving made by George Gibbs in 1850 indicates the caliber of this art, which is now lost (plate 106).

Some parts of the Plateau area have remained fairly conservative, and in almost every reservation a few women can be found who practice traditional crafts. Nez Percé and their neighbors still produce a limited number of twined baskets and wallets, but the material has changed from grass and corn husk to modern commercial yarns and jute string. Yarns with metallic fibers seem to be preferred in recent years. Typical imbricated baskets of good quality are made in several places, and they command high prices. A limited quantity of beadwork is still being made in the form of horse trappings, personal costumes, and especially rectangular women's bags with solidly beaded front panels, called "friendship bags." Twined wallets or beaded bags filled with roots are still standard gift items at intertribal gatherings. Much of this contemporary work, although made with new materials, is very much in traditional style. On the basis of style alone, it is often difficult to distinguish a new piece from one produced fifty years ago. Perhaps one of the reasons for this conservatism of design is that Plateau people have retained a fair number of old objects, and continually have them on hand as models.

94. Ghost Dance dress. Arapaho. Field Museum of Natural History, Chicago (Cat. No. 71950). Several dresses and men's shirts with very similar painted designs are known from the Arapaho. Note the use of the turtle as compared to plate 37.

95. Imbricated basket. Klickitat. Height 14⅜". Denver Art Museum (Cat. No. YKt 21)

96. Twined bag with false embroidery in corn husk and wool yarn. Nez Percé. 17½ x 14". Denver Art Museum (Cat. No. YNP–16). Collected by Grace Nicholson.

97. Elaborate horse gear at a modern powwow, showing a Yakima Indian woman of Satus Creek, Washington, at the Toppenish powwow, July, 1959. Photo courtesy of William L. Gannon, Mabton, Wash.

98. Twined basket wallet. Wasco. 7¾ x 7½". Denver Art Museum (Cat. No. YWas-1)

99. Bowl of mountain sheep horn. Wishram. Diameter 6″. Smithsonian Institution, Museum of Natural History, Washington, D.C. (Cat. No. 127860). Collected in 1886 by Charles Willoughby, the agent on the Quinault reservation.

100. Spoon of mountain sheep horn. Wishram. Length of figure on handle 3⅞″. Smithsonian Institution, Museum of Natural History, Washington, D.C. (Cat. No. 701). Collected by George Gibbs on the lower Columbia River before 1851.

101. Carved wood spoon. Wasco. Length 4¾″. Field Museum of Natural History, Chicago (Cat. No. 69089). Collected by M. L. Miller in 1901 at The Dalles, Oregon.

102. Carved wood figure. Wasco. Height 12″. Field Museum of Natural History, Chicago (Cat. No. 87603). Collected by Fred Harvey before 1905 on upper Memaloose Island.

103. *Shaman's* stick. Wasco. Height of carved section 9″. Field Museum of Natural History, Chicago (Cat. No. 87630.4). Collected by Fred Harvey before 1905 at The Dalles, Oregon.

104. Carved wood mortar. Wasco. Diameter 11½″. Field Museum of Natural History, Chicago (Cat. No. 87705). Collected by Fred Harvey before 1905 at The Dalles, Oregon.

105. Antler adze handle. Chinook (?). Length 8⅝″. Peabody Museum, Harvard University, Cambridge, Mass. (Cat. No. 67.9.10/139)

106. Prow of a Burial Canoe on the bank of the Columbia River at the mouth of Chamus Creek, Oct. 30, 1850. Sketch by George Gibbs. Smithsonian Institution, Museum of Natural History, Washington, D.C. This is an example of a rich art form which has not survived in our museum collections.

107. Blanket. Salish. Peabody Museum, Harvard University, Cambridge, Mass. (Cat. No. 97917). An example of a rare type of nobility blanket made by several Salish tribes. Early blankets of this type were supposedly made of dog hair.

Prow of dead Canoe on Bank of Columbia R. at mouth of Chamus creek. Oct 30 - 1850

THE PACIFIC NORTHWEST COAST

The Pacific coastline from Yakutat Bay in southeastern Alaska down to about the Columbia River is a clearly defined area with a distinct culture and art style, the influence of which extended as far as northern California. The area is fairly isolated by the abruptly rising Coast Range on the east. The waterways were the chief avenues of travel, with some access to the interior possible by way of the inland rivers to the south. In addition, the Tlingit and Tsimshian people had well-developed trails across the mountains for trade with the interior Athabascan groups.

In general, the area is characterized by a mild climate, thanks to the Japan current which warms much of the coastline, and by abundant rainfall. This combination has resulted in a dense vegetation with cedar, fir, and hemlock as common trees. The people lived along the rivers, or on the sheltered ocean inlets in the few places where a natural beach could be found. Although a little hunting was practiced in the forests, the people much preferred to stay close to the water. The sea became their main—and abundant—source of food. Fish of several varieties were regularly caught during spawning times, shell fish were gathered, and water mammals hunted. Wild plants and berries also contributed to a plentiful food supply. A very limited amount of agriculture in the form of tobacco farming was practiced in some areas, but no other crops were raised.

Because of the wealth of food, a good deal of leisure was available for a non-essential art industry, often a rare situation in a hunting–gathering economy. Wood and wood products were the main raw materials. Not only were the houses made of wood, but also storage boxes, food bowls, some spoons, and canoes. So also was ritual equipment, such as masks and rattles (plate 109; color, plates 5, 108, 113). Cedar bark was used for mats and clothing, and spruce roots for sewing and baskets. Other raw materials included animal products in the form of wool, skins, horn, bone, teeth, and ivory. There were also some stones, and seashells. Almost everything used by the Indians of this area was elaborately decorated, from the paint brushes and sewing awls, to the house posts and canoes. Artistically it was perhaps the most productive area in North America north of Mexico.

Rank was primarily based on ancestry and family connections in that the latter carried with them certain privileges, titles, names, and exclusive rights to certain dances, songs, rituals, and animal crests. However, each inherited privilege had to be validated at a *potlatch* in which guests were given gifts (actually payments for witnesses) which varied according to the importance of the privilege being validated and the rank of the recipient. Wealth in the form of material possessions was therefore an important prerequisite for achieving a high standing within the society. Efforts to raise one's social position consisted of acquiring wealth, and then holding a *potlatch* to validate an inherited privilege. To be an important individual on the Northwest Coast, it was first necessary to be "born right," that is, to have a defensible hereditary claim to high ranking privileges; and second, to have the necessary wealth to validate these privileges.

A certain degree of prestige could be achieved by well-known and skilled craftsmen who were continually called upon to create important carvings. *Shamans* who cured disease or predicted the future were also important personages, and they usually produced a specialized type of carving which was often of a particularly forceful character (color, plates 123, 124). Among the Kwakiutl and their neighbors, membership in secret societies assured prestige in that the right to membership was an inherited prerogative which was validated by lavish feasts and gift-giving.

Warfare was an important, if sporadic, activity in the Northern area. Sneak raids on neighboring tribes were common in order to acquire slaves or to avenge some supposed insult. Body armor was often elaborate, consisting of rod-and-slat jackets or heavy hides to protect the body, and wooden helmets and neck protectors in carved designs. A unique knife form was developed which was often pointed at both ends with a handle in the middle (plate 115). Daggers (plate 116), bows, and arrows were among the chief weapons, along with spears. Some Northern groups had the *atlatl* or spear-thrower, apparently borrowed from the Eskimo.

Ancestry was based on mythology about animals, and the art was therefore basically an expression of totemism. The people felt a direct and close relationship to mythological animals and used them as decoration on all of their clothing, houses, utensils, and of course the famous totem poles (plates 117, 118). The only non-totemic art was in the geometric treatment of designs on basketry and, occasionally, on woven garments. Some carving was quite realistic and actual portraiture was sometimes intended; but generally the art took the form of a series of conventionalizations. These included a type of symbolic presentation in which a whole animal, a beaver for example, was represented by the large incisor teeth and a large, usually cross-hatched tail; birds can be identified by the shape of their beaks, and other animals by the presence (or absence) of teeth, tongues, and tails. Some mythological animals are difficult to identify because land and sea animal characteristics are combined; thus, a "sea wolf" is shown as a typical conventionalized wolf, but with the addition of flippers. Important elements were sometimes enlarged for emphasis. Several conventions were developed specifically to permit the natural animal shape to conform to the form being decorated, especially among the Northern groups where there seemed to be

100

a horror of blank spaces. The representation of an animal figure might be split down the middle, both halves being shown attached to a common head. In addition, internal organs were sometimes shown in order to fill a space which would otherwise appear vacant. An eyelike element was often used at all joints, and occasionally faces or even complete animals were inserted within parts of a larger animal form.

It is fairly well demonstrable that the Northwest Coast art style had a flourishing tradition before Europeans arrived; however, early white contact produced a florescence of production. Not only were metal tools introduced in quantity, but also new materials—cloth, buttons, and copper (plates 120, 121). Most important, however, was the new opportunity for acquiring wealth opened up by the trade of furs and other services. Families of merely middle-class status were able to acquire sufficient possessions to compete in the *potlatches* with important chiefs. This new wealth accelerated the entire economy and vast quantities of carvings, totem poles, blankets, boxes, and other works of art were made from the late eighteenth century down to about the beginning of the twentieth century. About this time, the *potlatch* was outlawed by Canadian law, missionaries discouraged any Indian practices as being heathen, and whole villages became economically dependent upon commercial fishing—all factors which contributed to a decline in the arts.

Owing to the basically similar geographic terrain along the entire stretch of the coast, and the frequency of traveling and raiding, a basically similar cultural pattern subsisted throughout the area. There are, of course, many local differences even within tribal groups; each village was an independent unit and tribal unity was poorly developed. The art styles were determined rather by geographic proximity than by linguistic affiliation. For example, the northern Kwakiutl (Haisla) were more closely related to their Tsimshian neighbors than to the southern Kwakiutl. Likewise the northern Haida (Kaigani) showed many Tlingit characteristics, and the Salish-speaking Bella Coola resembled the central Kwakiutl more than any group of related Salishan Indians.

The Northwest Coast area can be roughly divided into three artistic areas, from north to south. The northern group, consisting of Tlingit, Haida, and Tsimshian, although showing many differences, are still closely related. Their sculpture is more refined than that of other areas, and more limited by the basic form of the material being decorated. Their totem poles, carved from a basically cylindrical tree form, have the figures wrapped around the curved surface so that the finished carving retains its cylindrical form. This contrasts with the southern style, in which added arms project from the carving and the space between the legs is sometimes completely cut through. Northern carving is usually finely finished and sometimes naturalistic, but always conforms rigidly to set conventions. The general feeling is of dignified restraint rather than freedom or boldness of form.

The Tsimshian, and especially the Tlingit, borrowed many elements of culture from the interior Athabascan tribes. They practiced such crafts as porcupine quillworking and beadwork in floral designs. They also used leather garments, and made skin moccasins. These two tribes were also famous for their woven goat hair and cedar bark blankets of the type known as "Chilkat." The name is derived from the Chilkat division of the Tlingit, which principally produced them during the historic period (plate 128). All the Northern groups produced very fine twined baskets in a basic pail shape, usually using spruce roots. Basketry hats and mats were also manufactured. A specialty of the Haida was the carving of miniature stone totem poles and novelties for the tourist trade; argillite, the material used, was only found in the Haida country near the town of Skidegate on the Queen Charlotte Islands. The Aleuts, living to the north of the Tlingit, also had some influences on Tlingit culture but little influence on their art, with the possible exception of the concept of adding extra faces and projections on some masks.

The Central Northwest Coast area is populated by the Kwakiutl and Bella Coola tribes, whose sculpture is bolder and less refined than that of the northern region. A clever carver could produce a fine texture, with rows of parallel adze marks running in different directions on different parts of the carving (color, plate 133). Masks from this area frequently have mechanical contrivances, or interchangeable parts, which enabled the wearers to completely change the character of the mask during a dramatic dance presentation. An identifying characteristic of carvings from this area is a rounded and projecting eye with a flattened pupil. Both the Bella Coola and Kwakiutl tended toward a bold use of paint, but in general Kwakiutl painting follows the lines of the carving, while the Bella Coola tended to paint across carved lines. Bella Coola also seem to prefer the use of a bright blue paint which became characteristic of the tribe's art (plates 129–31; color, plate 134; see also frontispiece).

Less basketry was produced in this area than in the other two, and little use was made of skin clothing. In the Kwakiutl area, there occurred the greatest development of secret societies, involving elaborate ritual and carvings connected with the ceremonies. Some, such as the Hamatsa or Cannibal Society, have received much notoriety because human flesh was evidently eaten during a portion of the ritual (color, plate 141). The Kwakiutl, though conscious of clan ancestry, placed somewhat less emphasis on clan crests than did the northern tribes.

The southern portion of the Northwest Coast area is comprised of the Coast Salish tribes, the Nootka, and lower Chinook. The people here had a greater dependence upon vegetable food, but also utilized sea products. The Nootka actually hunted whales on the open sea in their dugout canoes, and developed elaborate rituals around whale hunting. The sculpture in this

108. Clan hat. Tsimshian. National Museum of Canada, Ottawa (Cat. No. VII–C-1764)

area seems an indigenous development, but was considerably influenced from the north in comparatively recent times; in general, it is crude and simple, with a use of bright paint. A notable type made by the Nootka was a common form of mask, consisting of flat painted boards. The Nootka used these masks in their Wolf ritual.

Fine basketry in the twined technique is produced in this area by the Nootka Indians, while the Salishan groups used the imbricated coiled technique. Some Salish tribes produced a crude woven blanket of dog hair; early examples had elaborate geometric designs in polychrome twining, but later examples were simply white with a one-line red border.

The importance of the *potlatch* and the secret societies was replaced among the Coast Salish by an emphasis on personal guardian spirits, which spread as far south as the Columbia River. The most important carvings from this area took the form of guardian spirit figures, which were carried by some tribes in their spirit dances (plates 138–40).

Today there are no longer any wood-carvers among the northern tribes who have been trained in the traditional manner, that is, by serving an apprenticeship to a known craftsman. However, this is not true among the Kwakiutl who have maintained an unbroken tradition of fine craftsmanship along with a continuation of the *potlatch* system. The work of artists such as Charlie James, Willie Seaweed, and Mungo Martin are now eagerly sought after by both collectors and museums. There are also quite a few contemporary practicing artists who do excellent work. Some of the better-known artists are Henry Hunt, Tony Hunt, Charlie George, Jr., Charlie G. Walkus, Ed Walkus, and Doug Cranmer, to mention just a few. Bill Reid, a Haida artist, was not brought up in a wood-carving tradition but trained himself; he produces excellent work, including a reconstruction of a house and totem poles on the campus of the University of British Columbia at Vancouver. Bob Davidson, a young Haida, does fine work in wood, argillite, and silver under Bill Reid's tutelage.

The Indian Arts and Crafts Board is encouraging a few select carvers in Alaska by emphasizing creative effort rather than copying. Lincoln Wallace of Sitka, and Amos Wallace of Juneau are both doing fine Tlingit work. A project at Port Chilkoot, Alaska is helping to revive quality carvings among the Chilkat and in Nathan Jackson has produced a top rate artist. The Northwest Coast is indeed perhaps the only area where it is economically feasible to continue fine quality arts and crafts production in the old traditions.

Today there is a very limited production of Chilkat blankets. Baskets are still made at several places and the Nootkas still produce basketry of high quality. Carvings in bone, shell, and ivory, however, are no longer made, and there are only a very few Indians capable of engraving silver bracelets.

There are several non-Indians and Indians of tribes other than those from the Northwest Coast who produce Northwest Coast type carvings. It is a sign of the popularity of the style that carvings are produced by Seminole Indians in Florida in the form of totem poles—though these are not intended to fool anyone. Moreover, in recent years many obvious fakes have been placed on the market in an effort to meet the demands of collectors clamoring for examples of Northwest Coast art.

above: 109. Clan hat. Haida. Smithsonian Institution, Museum of Natural History, Washington, D.C. (Cat. No. 89037). Collected at Skidegate, Queen Charlotte Islands.

right: 110. Carved standing figure (front). Tlingit. Height 61″. American Museum of Natural History, New York City (Cat. No. E 1915). From a *shaman's* grave house.

far right: 111. Back view of figure in plate 110

112. Face mask. Chilkat Tlingit. American Museum of Natural History, New York City (Cat. No. 19/854). Collected by George Emmons before 1890.

113. Bird mask with movable beak. Probably Haida. Carnegie Museum, Pittsburgh. Fred Harvey Collection (Cat. No. 3178/30)

114. Face mask. Chilkat Tlingit. Height 9⅜″. Smithsonian Institution, Museum of Natural History, Washington, D.C. (Cat. No. 76855). Collected by T. Dix Bolles before 1885. Chinese temple coins for eyes and opercula for teeth.

right: 115. Fighting knife. Tlingit. Length 22¾″. University Museum, Philadelphia (Cat. No. 42–30–42)

far right: 116. Iron dagger. Tlingit. Length 21¼″. Denver Art Museum (Cat. No. QT1–3)

117. Totem pole (front). Haida. Height 20'10". University Museum, Philadelphia (Cat. No. 37728 and 29–47–201). Collected by C. F. Newcombe at Masset, Queen Charlotte Islands, in 1900.

118. Side view of pole in plate 117

119. Button blanket. Tsimshian. 50¾ x 74⅜". University Museum, Philadelphia (Cat. No. NA 8516). Collected by Louis Shotridge on the Nass River in British Columbia, 1918.

120. Cloth appliqué shirt (front). Haida (?). Royal Ontario Museum, University of Toronto, Canada (Cat. No. HN 894). A double-headed wolf is shown on the front.

121. Back view of shirt in plate 121, showing a shark

122. The interior of the Whale House at Klukwan, Alaska. Chilkat Tlingit. Note the beautifully carved and painted wall screen and the house posts. The old Whale House is no longer standing, but the screen and house posts are still preserved by the Chilkat at Klukwan.

123. *Shaman's* mask of a wolf, according to George Emmons. Tlingit. Height 10". American Museum of Natural History, New York City (Cat. No. 19/853). Collected by George Emmons from a Chilkat grave. Opercula teeth and metal eye.

124. *Shaman's* crown. Tlingit. Height 6¾". American Museum of Natural History, New York City (Cat. No. E 2350). Collected by George Emmons at Klukwan, Alaska. Human hair, feathers, bird skin, blue jay feathers, and bearskin.

125. Panel from a house platform. Tlingit. American Museum of Natural History, New York City (Cat. No. E 1385). Collected by George Emmons from an old Kar-gwan-ton House at Sitka, Alaska. Represents a bear with opercula for teeth.

126. Face mask. Heiltsuk (Bella Bella). American Museum of Natural History, New York City (Cat. No. 16/594). Abalone shell inlay. From the Bishop Collection and purchased in 1888.

127. Painted skin shirt. Tsimshian. Museum of the American Indian, Heye Foundation, New York City.

128. Chilkat blanket. Tlingit. Field Museum of Natural History, Chicago (Cat. No. 19571)

129. Headdress. Bella Coola. 10⅞ x 6⅞". Private collection. Compare the carving on the headdress frontals of plates 130, 131, and 134 to note differences in tribal styles.

below: 130. Headdress. Tsimshian. Royal Ontario Museum, University of Toronto, Canada (Cat. No. HN 910). Collected on the Nass River by Charles Marius Barbeau.

below right: 131. Headdress. Haida (?). 7¼ x 5½". Private collection. Collected from the Kwakiutl at Alert Bay, but not of Kwakiutl manufacture.

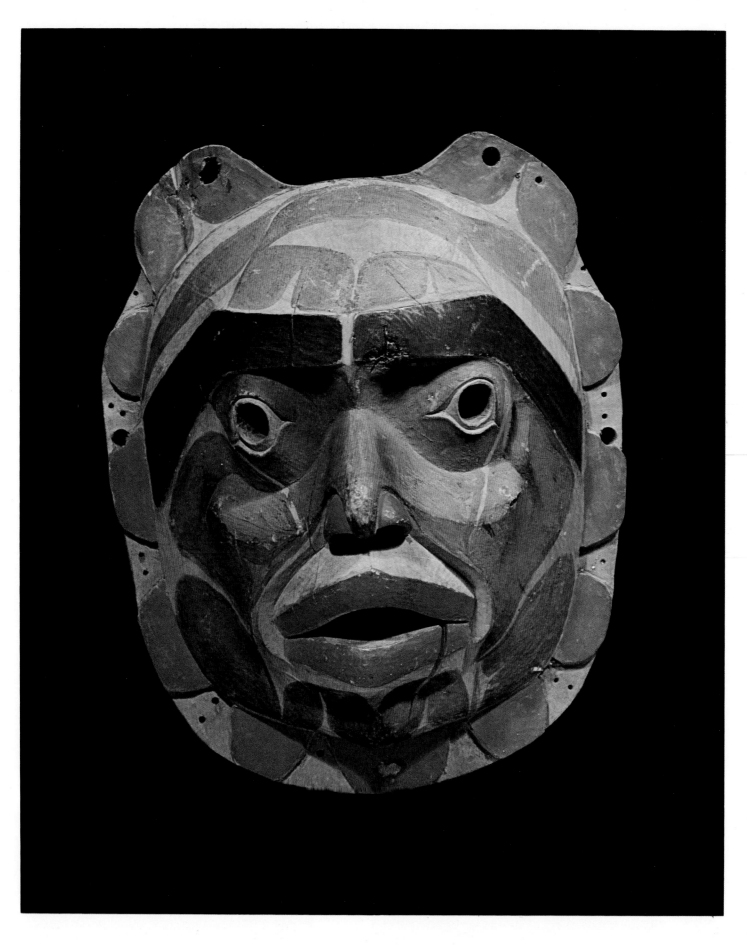

132. Face mask. Bella Coola. Height 14½″. American Museum of Natural History, New York City (Cat. No. 16/596)

133. Wolf mask. Kwakiutl (?). 7¼ x 20¼″. Denver Art Museum (Cat. No. NNu–7). A very old and very finely carved mask. Note the detailed adzing.

134. Headdress. Bella Bella. 8¼ x 7¾″. Collection John Hauberg, Seattle, Wash. An extremely fine and old example with copper inlay in place of the usual abalone shell inlay.

115

135. Face mask. Kwakiutl.
11⅞ x 9¼". Private collection.
Represents Tsonoqua, a
cannibal woman.

below left: 136. Face mask. Kwakiutl. Height
12¼". Milwaukee Public Museum, Wisconsin.
Anthropology Collection (Cat. No. 17357). A
version of the Wild Man mask, collected by
S. A. Barrett in 1915.

below right: 137. Face mask. Kwakiutl.
Height 10⅞". Denver Art Museum (Cat.
No. NKw–39–P). Another variation on the
Wild Man theme.

138. Guardian spirit figure.
Snoqualmie (?). Height 25¾″.
Denver Art Museum (Cat.
No. QS1–1)

139. Face mask. Cowichan.
Denver Art Museum (Cat.
No. NCow–1). Collected by
George Emmons in 1935 at
Duncan, British Columbia.
The mask, called Swaixwe,
represents a guardian spirit.

140. Spindle whorls. Cowichan. Smithsonian Institution, Museum of Natural
History, Washington, D. C. (Cat. Nos. 221, 179b, and c.). Collected on Vancouver
Island.

141. Dance mask. Kwakiutl. 21 x 51″. Denver Art Museum (Cat. No. NKw–25).
A four-headed mask for use in the Hamatsa (Cannibal) Society Dances. Carved
by George Walkus of Blunden Harbor, British Columbia, in 1938.

118

The Arctic Coast

The Woodlands

THE ARCTIC COAST

The Arctic Coast from the Aleutian Islands to eastern Greenland is the home of a group of people racially quite distinct from American Indians to the south. Although the Eskimo have inhabited the area for at least two thousand years, they are comparative newcomers to the North American continent, and still bear close cultural affinities to parts of eastern Siberia. The Arctic Coast is a vast area; nevertheless, the Eskimo living on Greenland are not very different culturally from those in western Alaska, and they are also related linguistically.

The normal economic pattern for Eskimo groups consists of seasonal migrations on land in the summer to hunt caribou, musk ox, and polar bear, in addition to doing some fishing, and on or near the sea during the winter when seal and walrus are hunted through their breathing holes in the ice. Some Eskimo groups, such as those around Point Hope, Alaska, are also proficient whalers.

Geographically and climatically the area is inhospitable, with long, cold, dark winters and short summers. The Eskimo made an amazing adaptation to this difficult environment. House types varied. They included the familiar dome-shaped igloo built of snow blocks, simple skin-covered tents, and fairly permanent, earth-covered semi-subterranean structures. Clothing, made of a variety of skins with or without fur, was more tailored than anywhere else north of Mexico. Transportation was accomplished by dog sled in winter, and in summer by skin-covered canoes, these being the smaller enclosed boat known as a kayak, and the larger open vessel known as an umiak.

The harsh conditions in which these people lived were eased by social attitudes in which food and shelter became in effect communal property. Each individual was willing to share whatever resources he had, in the realization that at some future time his own survival might depend upon someone else's sharing with him. It was also the custom, in difficult times, to practice infanticide and abandonment of the lame or aged which, however barbaric to our society, was necessary in the Arctic.

Religious practices were somewhat rudimentary, but a rich mythology concerning the animals hunted was evolved, and a host of taboos and restrictions were followed. *Shamans* had the important responsibilities of curing disease, controlling the weather, and insuring an adequate food supply. In some areas the people gathered once a year for ceremonies in which masked dancers impersonated gods and spirits. The masks worn on these occasions are perhaps the most striking form of art produced in this area; they occur in great variety (plates 142, 145–47; color, plate 143). In their most characteristic shape, they have small appendages attached around the perimeter, in the form of hands, feet, fish, clams, and seals. Real feathers are also attached. The older masks are made of pieces of driftwood and are painted in dull polychrome. A type of plain face mask without appendages was also common.

Since the area is so poor in natural resources, it is surprising to find the Eskimo artistically productive. Wood is not available in some regions; walrus ivory, horn, bone, and stone have, however, taken its place. Even native copper was used where it was available. Some of the Eskimo inventions included the bow drill, snow goggles, harpoons, dog sleds, stone oil lamps, and a moon-shaped type of woman's knife. They produced no weaving, but made a type of coiled basket in some areas—perhaps a recent introduction due to external influence. A crude form of pottery was formerly produced, but generally more stable materials than clay were preferred.

The earliest prehistoric Eskimo remains show a fully developed artistic tradition of carving in ivory and slate. In the historic period, the Eskimo have continued to excel in ivory carving, but now produce mostly objects for resale: small carvings of animals and birds are common, as are ivory pipes, cribbage boards, jewelry, buttons, buckles, and needle cases. Some of these larger ivory carvings have naive, scratched engravings showing hunting or boating scenes, or simple geometric designs which have survived from prehistoric periods. Early efforts at encouraging Eskimo artistic production have developed new crafts, including painting on parchment in imitation of engraving on ivory. Wooden bowls were also produced with imaginative paintings of mythological animals (plate 148) and, of course, reproductions of wood masks were made for sale. Masks of whalebone are being made, for resale, in an old tradition, as well as masks of fur made in Alaska but copied from those of an old Labrador Eskimo tradition. Recent years have seen the considerable commercial success of brand new arts which have little or no basis in tradition, but which are nevertheless very much in the Eskimo character: carvings in soapstone, and prints made from soapstone blocks or skin stencils. Sale of both prints and soapstone carvings has met with phenomenal success, and experiments with new techniques will probably follow.

The Aleut groups who inhabited the Aleutian Islands were linguistically related to the Eskimo, but their culture was somewhat different, owing to a different environment. They lived in an area where there was little snow and ice, and so could remain on land in permanent villages all winter. They shared many traits with their Eskimo kinsmen, such as the harpoon hunting of seals from kayaks. They also borrowed many elements of social culture from the Northwest Coast groups. Having class distinctions and slaves, they were notable for making flexible baskets which are among the very finest in the world. Aleut men wore a distinctive type of visor hat—bent wood, painted

122

in polychrome, with attachments in the form of sea lion whiskers, beads, and carved ivory ornaments (color, plates 144, 149).

Aleut culture was early destroyed by Russian fur traders who employed the men on their voyages, and no distinctive Aleut crafts are being manufactured today.

142. Mask. Eskimo. Maximum width 28″. Milwaukee Public Museum, Wisconsin. Anthropology Collection (Cat. No. 16477/4356). Collected at Goodnews Bay, on the southwest coast of Alaska.

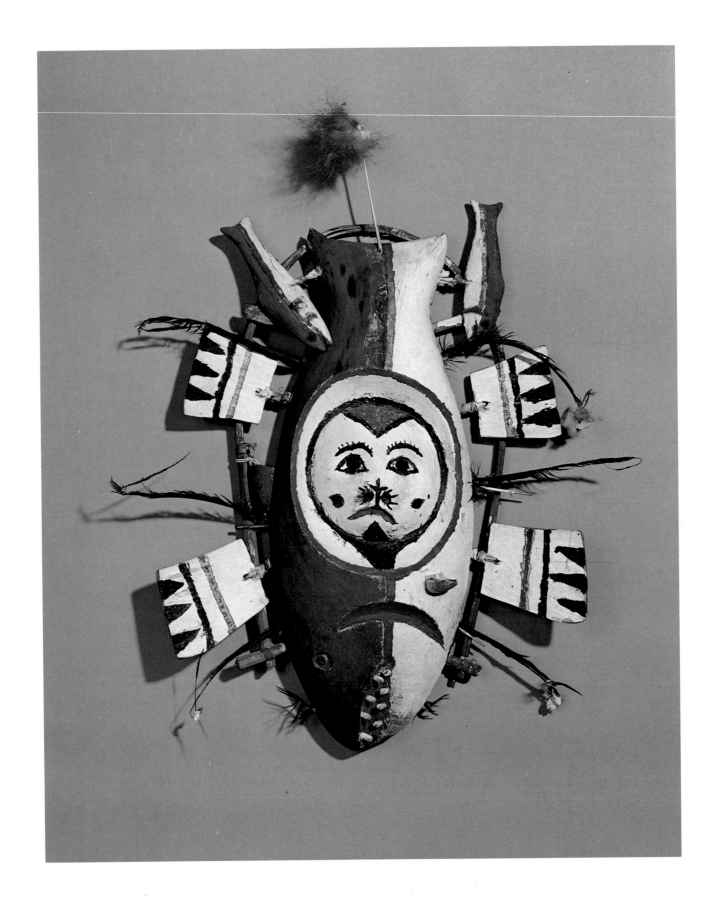

143. Mask. Eskimo. 14½ x 12½". Denver Art Museum (Cat. No. P–105–25–E)

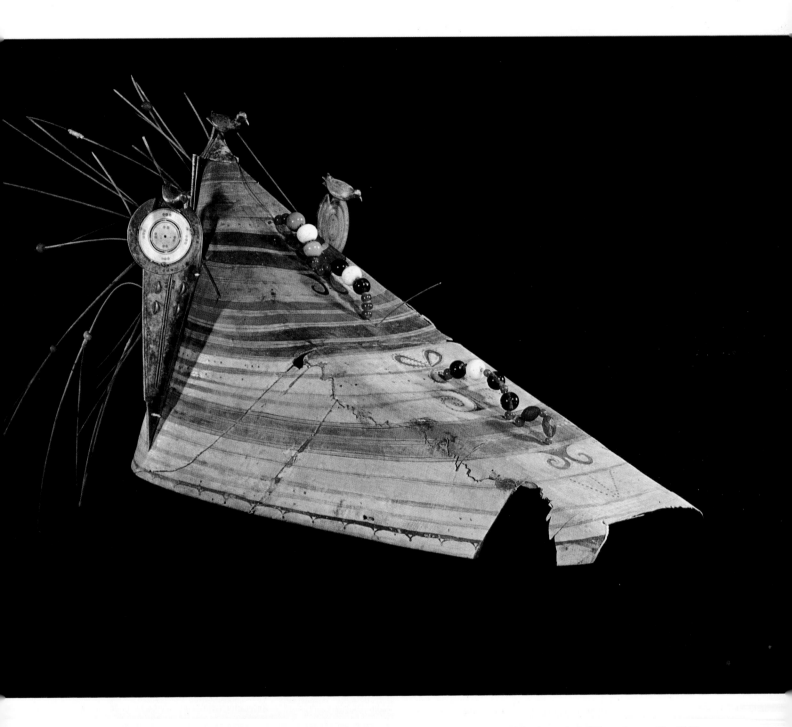

144. Hat. Aleut. Peabody Museum, Salem, Mass. (Cat. No. E3486). Collected by Captain William Osgood in 1829.

145. Mask. Eskimo. 23⅝ x 7″.
Denver Art Museum (Cat. No.
NEsk–27). From Nunivak Island,
Alaska.

146. Mask. Eskimo. Height 17″.
Denver Art Museum (Cat. No.
NEsk–1)

147. Two small masks. Eskimo. Peabody
Museum, Salem, Mass. (Cat. Nos. 13091 and
13082)

148. Painted wood bowl. Eskimo. 7½ x 12¼″. Denver Art
Museum (Cat. No. QEsk–58). Collected by Edward S. Curtis.

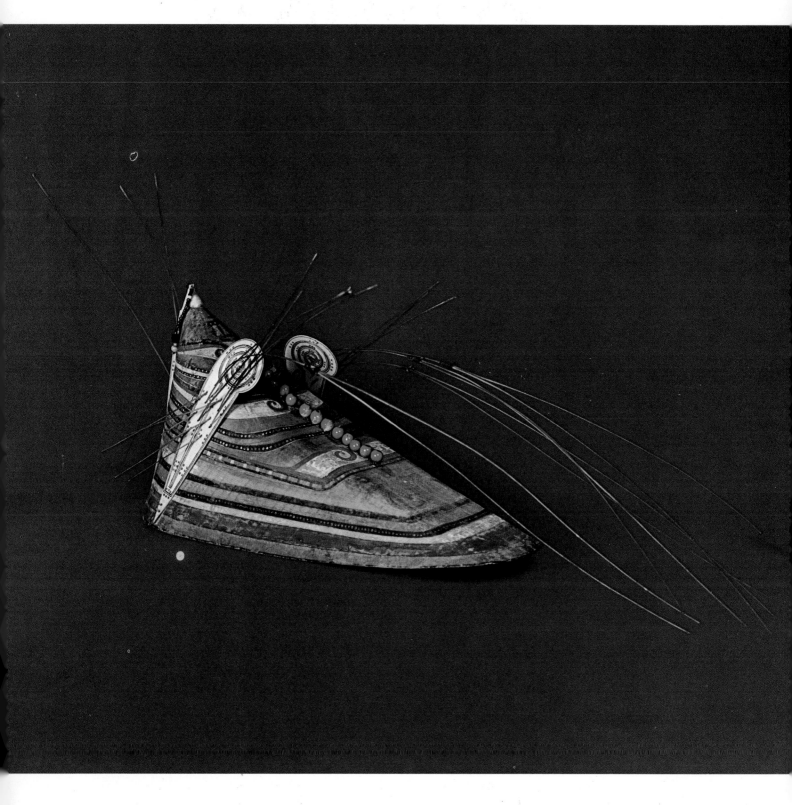

149. Wood hat. Aleut. Length 16½″. Museum of the American Indian, Heye Foundation, New York City (Cat. No. 14/4869). Painted wood with glass trade beads, carved ivory, and walrus whiskers.

THE WOODLANDS

The entire area from the interior of Canada and Alaska to the Atlantic Coast, and all of the United States east of the Mississippi River is, for convenience, discussed here as one area; except in the far north, the area is characterized by deciduous forests. In general, the Indian inhabitants derived at least a portion of their food supply from corn farming, but the cultures of this vast area, although they showed superficial similarities, were certainly not homogeneous. As a culture area, the Woodlands therefore is considered as divisible into four distinct subareas: the Northern Woodlands, the Great Lakes area, the Northeast, and the Southeast.

The Northern Woodlands runs just south of the Eskimo area through Alaska and Canada, and forms a sparsely settled region covered with evergreen forests. The people may be divided into two major divisions: Athabascans to the west, and Algonkian-speaking people to the east. Farming was not practiced here; the economy was based on seasonal hunting and gathering, and almost everywhere famine alternated with plenty. The arts were poorly developed. The lives of these people were affected almost immediately upon first contact with Europeans. They soon became dependent upon the fur trade and trade goods. Rifles and steel traps took the place of their bows and arrows, flour and bacon replaced wild game. They adopted Christianity, and much of their old material culture completely disappeared.

Influences from neighboring tribes had previously caused variations in their culture. In the west, the Carrier and Tahltan were influenced by Northwest Coast peoples; the Naskapi, Kutchin, Ingalik, and Chipewyan showed many traits borrowed from the Eskimo; Plains Cree and Bungi showed Plains characteristics; and Ojibwa living north of the Great Lakes showed influences from that area. Almost everywhere in this vast region the Indians made bark vessels, utilizing birch, elm, or spruce. Bark was also useful for sheathing canoes, and some groups even covered their houses with it. Thin laces of rawhide known as *babiche* were used to construct bags and to lace snowshoes. Other crafts included the making of some splint and wicker baskets, wood carving of spoons and bowls, and simple weaving of rabbit skin blankets, as well as twined bags and burden straps. Pottery was unknown.

Garments were often fitted in a style perhaps borrowed from the Eskimo and decorated with porcupine quill or moose-hair embroidery. The Naskapi used elaborate painted decoration on their garments as late as the beginning of the twentieth century (plate 150). This type of painting must have been

129

more widespread in the precontact period, but was generally replaced by decoration in brightly colored quills and glass beads. The quill and moose-hair embroidery produced in this area was some of the finest made anywhere, and was remarkable for delicacy of line, fine stitching, and technical excellence. A small amount is still being produced, but most of the workers prefer to use silk embroidery thread rather than porcupine quills.

Lake Michigan is the center of the Great Lakes area. Here the abundance of water, game, and hard wood forests helped to shape the pattern of living: the people lived very much like those of the Northern Woodlands but, in addition to seasonal hunting and gathering, practiced corn farming, gathered wild rice as a staple food, and made a greater use of fish and small game than the northerners. Relatively sedentary, they not only built fairly large villages around their corn fields, but often maintained separate villages for the winter season.

Owing to their abundant and easily obtainable food supply, and the sedentary pattern of life, they were able to develop a more complex religious system and more refined arts than those of the Northern Woodlands, which, in general, they resemble. Again, bark was commonly used for containers, canoes, and for covering the conical or dome-shaped wigwams. The Great Lakes people also used sonwshoes and toboggans, made plaited baskets, twined bags, and decorated clothing with porcupine quillwork. However, there are of course many differences between the cultures. Folded rawhide boxes took the place of *babiche* bags, quills completely replaced moose hair for embroidery, and work in wool and yarn was more highly developed (plate 151; color, plates 157, 158). Above all, they used wood, making a great variety of finely carved wooden bowls, spoons, war clubs, and dolls for use in medicine bundles (plates 160, 161). Indeed, although they carved no masks, the Great Lakes people ranked second in wood carving only to the Northwest Coast Indians.

Some of the more distinctive features of Great Lakes art are to be found in their ribbon appliqué (colorplate 166). Silk ribbons in assorted widths and colors were traded or given as gifts as early as were glass beads. The former were sewn to bags and garments as edge trim, or cut and folded into designs applied to the object being decorated. Sometimes dozens of narrow ribbons would be overlapped to produce wide bands of design which were then applied to women's skirts or blankets. The use of ribbon for decoration was widespread, but was brought to its highest development in this area.

Great Lakes people also excelled in the art of embroidering with porcupine quills (color, plate 167). They developed native dyes which produced bright, long-lasting colors, and sewed the dyed quills onto leather often smoked a rich brown, or dyed a brown black color, the better to accentuate the richly colored quills. Early quillwork often took the form of designs worked in triangles, but floral designs are also known.

When commercial woolen cloths were introduced, the Indians seemed to favor dark blue or black for decoration with colored glass beads. The Ojibwa developed a distinctive style, using naturalistic floral designs on black velvet; other Great Lakes tribes used more abstract floral designs on black wool cloth. Although Great Lakes Indians seemed to prefer floral designs for appliquéd beadwork, their loomed beadwork was usually in geometric patterns. Ribbon appliqué could be in either floral or geometric designs, but a widespread style was very much like some early triangular quillwork patterns.

Metal ornaments were produced by all Great Lakes tribes, and as elsewhere, were made in imitation of earlier trade pieces. A certain amount was produced from hammered coins, but the great bulk of it was made after 1860 from flat sheets of nickel silver. The most common ornament was a perforated brooch used on women's garments; there were also finger rings, earrings, bracelets, hat bands, head bands, and women's combs.

The Midéwiwin or Grand Medicine Society, a secret curing society which supposedly endowed members with supernatural powers, was the dominant religion. Membership was gained by purchasing initiation into the different degrees by gifts and feasts. The ritual and paraphernalia were elaborate, and a form of picture writing was developed as a memory aid to recall the songs and ritual sequence (plate 169). The medicine bags associated with this society were passed down from generation to generation; they are some of the oldest examples of Indian objects still retained by living Indians. All Great Lakes tribes kept a variety of sacred medicine bundles, which often contained ancient treasures. Bundles were kept for warding off disease, for luck in love, or for success in war. Some were clan property, other belonged to individuals; some were made up following a dream-vision which directed how the bundle should be made and what it should contain, but others simply contained relics of important chiefs. Bundles are still owned by many Indians in this area and the Grand Medicine Society is active in a few places. In some tribes the Drum religion has replaced the Midéwiwin, and in others, Peyote (Native American Church) or Christianity is the dominant religion.

Much cross-cultural influence affected the Great Lakes and neighboring areas. The Ojibwa influenced groups to the north, especially the related Plains Ojibwa and Cree, in the production of naturalistic floral designs. Many Great Lakes groups were pushed out into the prairies, assuming Plains characteristics in their new environments. Groups such as the Nebraska Winnebago, Iowa, Prairie Potawatomi, and Santee Sioux all shared both Woodland and Plains traits. In addition, the displacements and migrations which sent some Great Lakes tribes to resettle in the Prairies also caused some Northeastern Woodland groups to move west into the Great Lakes area. Wisconsin became the new home for scattered Oneida, Stockbridge, Brotherton, and Munsee groups, which certainly brought Eastern influences with them.

A few craft workers remain. Although their production is limited, some is in the old, fine tradition. Metalwork, wood carving, quill embroidery, and skin tanning are no longer viable crafts; but a few women still make yarn sashes and twined bags, good ribbon appliqué, and bead decoration.

The Northeastern Woodlands area runs from the eastern Great Lakes through New York and New England. At the time of first contact by Europeans, it was occupied with a great many tribes of the Algonkian stock, and the powerful Iroquois confederacy. Little is known about most of the Atlantic Coast groups because of their early extinction by disease and by warfare with Indians and whites alike. They seem to have had a culture much resembling that of the Great Lakes area, although lacking wild rice and the Midéwiwin religion. The Coast tribes depended upon seafoods to a great extent, but were also corn farmers and hunters.

The Iroquois are a conservative group still occupying much the same territory as they did on first contact. They live today on scattered reservations in New York State and Canada, and have maintained a surprising amount of their culture in spite of their having been so early exposed to white contact. Many Iroquois still speak their own language, follow the religious teachings of their prophet "Handsome Lake," participate in masked dances, and maintain some old arts. The political organization of the Iroquois—a confederation of six tribes, with the women having a strong voice in major policy making—is well known, and the model which held the Oneida, Seneca, Mohawk, Onondaga, Cayuga, and Tuscarora together in the League of the Iroquois was supposedly followed in framing the Constitution of the United States. Always an important military power, the Iroquois also expertly controlled trade over a wide area, and forced the removal of some of the Eastern Algonkian groups. Their alliance was eagerly sought by the Dutch, the English, and later by the United States.

Northeastern tribes, and especially the Iroquois, were similar in material culture to Great Lakes people (plates 171–73, 178; color, plate 168). Splint basketry had its greatest development in this area; wood carving was highly developed; yarn sashes, twined bags, and metal ornaments were made. Bark containers differed from those of the Great Lakes in that elm bark was used more commonly than birch. The typical Iroquois home was a long rectangular structure covered with sheets of elm bark. The Iroquois received a larger quantity of trade silver ornaments than Great Lakes groups because of their proximity to early settlers, and thus developed more advanced techniques of metalworking. Iroquois worked with real silver, rather than with nickel silver, and learned to run it into molds as well as pound out coins into flat shapes. In early historic times the Iroquois were potters, but their ware was soon replaced by traded metal utensils. Leather garments were replaced at

132

an early date by imported cloth, as happened everywhere in the eastern United States. The Iroquois developed a distinctive beadwork style consisting of light, lacy designs worked mostly in white beads on a dark cloth background.

Perhaps the most spectacular works produced by the Iroquois are their wooden masks, worn in curing ceremonies (plates 179, 180; color, plate 174). These false face masks are carved from living trees, and those actually used in ceremonies are believed to possess animate spirits. Small packets of tobacco are tied to their hair, they are fed regularly, and when not in use are carefully wrapped in clean white cloths and put away face down. These masks take a great variety of shapes[15] depending in part upon what role they are intended to play in the ceremonies. They are painted in black, red, or sometimes a combination of both. More recent examples often have white paint in addition to the black and red. Other trim includes circular metal eyes, horsehair, and corn husks on a few examples.

The Delaware tribe, neighbors of the Iroquois to the south, also made masks but, owing to early displacement and acculturation, few examples have survived (color, plate 175).

Some traditional Iroquois crafts are still very much alive. Although no metalwork, woven sashes, or twined bags are being produced, wood carving is actively carried on: spoons, bowls, stirring paddles, and canes are made, in addition to masks. Several women still make corn husk masks and dress corn husk dolls, while others produce splint baskets.

The entire southern part of the United States, form Texas to the Atlantic Ocean, comprises what is the Southeastern area. This part of the country, in prehistoric times, could boast the highest development of native American civilization north of Mexico. Huge earth mounds, elaborate artistic production, sun worship, royal families, and large cities were features of it, which probably owed their forms to influences from Mexico. Some groups, like the Natchez, still showed evidences of this higher civilization when first encountered by Europeans, but a decline had begun long before. The entire Southeast was subsequently strongly affected by European settlement in their area; entire tribes became extinct owing to war and new diseases, while others adopted the white man's ways. The so-called Five Civilized Tribes—Cherokee, Choctaw, Creek, Chickasaw, and Seminole—very early adopted European clothing, and went on to organize their own universities and newspapers. The invention of a Cherokee alphabet by Sequoya in 1821 facilitated this process of acculturation. Most of the Five Civilized Tribes moved to the Oklahoma area by 1830, leaving only a few scattered groups in the Southeast.

Early Southeastern products included finely made pottery with designs in a scroll pattern either painted or incised. A special type of beaded belt or shoulder sash was made with a very similar scroll design. Baskets were commonly made in split and plaited cane, and formerly feather capes were produced. Southeastern Indians made some of the most complex yarn sashes to be found anywhere; some, with beads worked into the design, are technically more accomplished than anything produced in the Great Lakes or Northeastern areas. There are also a few early examples of shoulder bags with beaded straps and triangular flap pouches (color, plate 176). These are often done in very fine beads, but the designs usually look like random wandering lines.

Simple silverwork was produced by most groups, but the ornaments were quite crude in comparison to those made by the Iroquois. The Seminole developed a distinctive type in the form of flat plaques, with cutout designs, to decorate women's capes. In general, however, little is known about early Southeastern crafts because so little has survived from the preacculturation period.

Recent Southeastern crafts include a continuation, among several groups, of the fine basketry tradition. Most notable are the Chitimacha who produced fine cane baskets, sometimes employing a double weave. The Seminole in Florida now specialize in a type of patchwork decoration on skirts and jackets for sale to tourists (color, plate 177). It is made by sewing, cutting, and resewing small scraps of differently colored cloth into geometric patterns. The work is done on a sewing machine, often hand-cranked in remote parts of the Florida Everglades!

A few groups, such as the Cherokee and Catawba, still produce a little pottery for sale; the Cherokee in North Carolina have generally maintained a considerable production, for the tourist trade, of split baskets, blow guns, and wooden masks, as well as such non-traditional items as wooden figures and handspun woolen cloths.

150. Painted skin masks. Naskapi. Each approximately 9¼ x 8⅛″. Denver Art Museum (Cat. Nos. NNE–3 and 5). Both collected by Dr. Frank G. Speck.

151. Twined bag. Stockbridge (?).
11½ x 15″. State Historical
Society of Wisconsin, Madison
(Cat No. 1954.2048)

152. Tobacco cutting board.
Winnebago. 7¼ x 7½″. Denver Art
Museum (Cat. No. QB1–118). The
incised design is of two otters.

153. Wood pipe bowl. Ojibwa.
Minnesota Historical Society, St.
Paul (Cat. No. E 98). A pipe stem
fits in the neck, and the top of the
head is the pipe bowl. Brass tacks
for eyes and near ears.

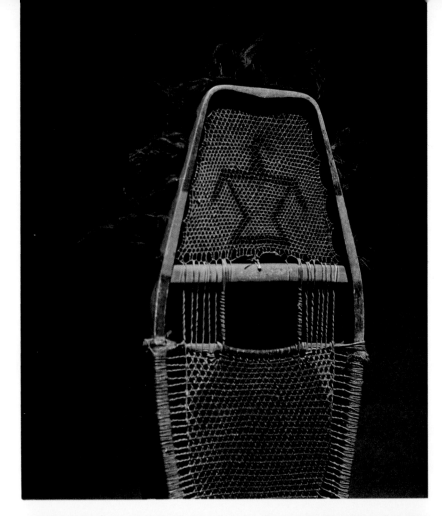

154. Snowshoe. Chippewa. Cranbrook Institute of Science, Bloomfield Hills, Michigan. This shows a painted thunderbird on the webbing of the toe.

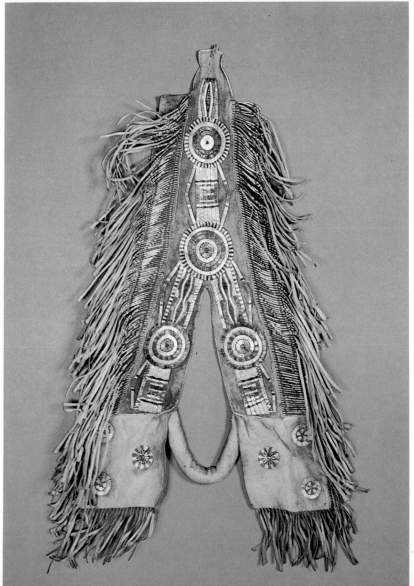

155. Crupper for horse. Cree. Length 30″. Museum of the American Indian, Heye Foundation, New York City (Cat. No. 18/5498). Made of porcupine quills.

above left: 156. Man's hood.
Tribe unknown. Royal
Ontario Museum, University
of Toronto, Canada (Cat. No.
916.22.1)

above: 157. Yarn belt.
Menominee. 100 x 15".
American Museum of Natural
History, New York City (Cat.
No. 50/9797). Made of
commercial yarn in a
finger-braiding technique.

left; 158. Twined bag. Sauk.
Oklahoma. 20½ x 30".
Denver Art Museum (Cat.
No. RSF–10)

137

159. Carved saddle. Menominee. American Museum of Natural History, New York City (Cat. No. 50/4848). Collected in 1910 by Alanson Skinner. Carved of wood and covered with rawhide. The carved horse head on the pommel was a specialty of the Menominee and some of their neighbors.

160. Wood bowl. Winnebago. Diameter 6¾″. Denver Art Museum (Cat. No. QWin–1)

161. Wood bowl. Kaskaskia (?). Peabody Museum, Harvard University, Cambridge, Mass. (Cat. No. 52998)

162. Antler war club.
Winnebago. Length 15½″.
University Museum,
Philadelphia (Cat. No.
62.32.1). Collected by Caleb
Pusy in 1839 at Fort
Winnebago. The other side
has a glass mirror inset.

163. Juggler's doll. Ojibwa. Height
17″. Milwaukee Public Museum,
Wisconsin. Anthropology Collection
(Cat. No. 55324)

164. Pair of wood dolls. Ojibwa.
Royal Ontario Museum, University
of Toronto, Canada (Cat. Nos.
HD12611 and 12608). Used in rites
of the Grand Medicine Society.

165. Pair of dolls. Menominee.
Milwaukee Public Museum,
Wisconsin. Anthropology Collection
(Cat. No. 24991). Collected by S. A.
Barrett in 1919. Used to perform
magic tricks.

166. Man's moccasins. Miami.
c. 1850–75. Length 9½". Cranbrook
Institute of Science, Bloomfield
Hills, Michigan (Cat. No. 3053). Silk
ribbon appliqué on flaps.

167. Quilled pouch. Mesquakie
(Fox). Collection Milford G.
Chandler, Detroit. The bottom
portion is the skin of a mallard
duck.

168. Quilled birchbark box.
Micmac. 10½ x 8½". Denver Art
Museum (Cat. No. VMi–12)

169. Incised birchbark scroll (detail). Ojibwa. Size of entire scroll 71¾ x 15¾". Denver Art Museum (Cat. No. Coj–36). Collected by A. G. Heath in 1915 from Chief Jim Greenhill at Cass Lake, Minnesota. These scrolls are used as memory aids in the performance of the ceremonies of the Grand Medicine Society.

170. Beaded charms. Ojibwa. Larger charm, 9½ x 7⅜"; smaller charm, 7¾ x 6". Denver Art Museum (Cat. Nos. BOj–24 and 23). These are worn as health charms by members of the Grand Medicine Society. Small shells are sewn in pockets behind the hands, feet, and head.

171. Carved wood pipe with
lead-lined bowl. Rhode Island (?).
Smithsonian Institution,
Museum of Natural History,
Washington, D.C. (Cat. No.
10080). Collected by George
Gibbs.

172. Ball-headed war club.
Mohawk (?). Skokloster
Castle, Sweden. Supposedly
collected before 1676. The
club is inlaid with purple and
white shell wampum.

173. Quilled black buckskin
bag. Delaware (?). c. 1775.
20½ x 5¾". Denver Art
Museum (Cat. No. VA1–2).
An old bag with no collection
history.

174. False face mask. Cayuga. 1860. Height 11½". Museum of the American Indian, Heye Foundation, New York City (Cat. No. 21/8246)

175. Wood face mask. Delaware. Length with fur drop 28". Museum of the American Indian, Heye Foundation, New York City (Cat. No. 2/814)

144

176. Beaded shoulder pouch. Seminole (?). Pouch 8⅜ x 7½". Field Museum of Natural History, Chicago (Cat. No. 258646). The design of a man on the pouch flap is unusual.

177. Man's patchwork shirt and skirt. Seminole. Length 56". Denver Art Museum (Cat. No. RSe–1)

178. Wampum belt. Huron. 4 x 22″. Smithsonian Institution, Museum of Natural History, Washington, D.C. (Cat. No. 165, 103). Collected by William Welles Thompson in 1892. The so-called Confederation belt.

179. Cayuga man wearing a false face mask and carrying a turtle-shell rattle. Photo by M. R. Harrington on the Grand River reservation, Canada, 1907. Photo courtesy of the Museum of the American Indian, New York City.

180. False face mask. Oneida. Height 10¼″. Milwaukee Public Museum, Wisconsin. Anthropology Collection (Cat. No. 3242). Collected by T. R. Roddy in 1906 in Canada.

Notes

1 John Sloan and Oliver La Farge, *Introduction to American Indian Art*, New York, 1931.

2 Robert T. Davis, *Native Arts of the Pacific Northwest*, Stanford, 1949, and Robert B. Inverarity, *Art of the Northwest Coast Indians*, Berkeley, 1950.

3 Frederick J. Dockstader, "The Kachina and the White Man," *Cranbrook Institute of Science Bulletin*, No. 35, 1954.

4 Alice Marriott, *Maria: The Potter of San Ildefonso*, Norman, 1948.

5 James Howard, "Pan-Indian Culture of Oklahoma," *The Scientific Monthly*, November, 1955, pp. 215–20.

6 Alice Marriott, "The Trade Guild of Southern Cheyenne Women," *Bulletin of the Oklahoma Anthropological Society*, Vol. IV, April, 1956, pp. 19–27.

7 For further details on culture areas, see Clark Wissler, *The American Indian*, New York, 1938, and Alfred L. Kroeber, *Cultural and Natural Areas of Native North America*, Berkeley, 1939.

8 John C. Ewers, *Plains Indian Painting*, Stanford, 1939.

9 John C. Ewers and William Wildschut, *Crow Indian Medicine Bundles* (Museum of the American Indian, Contributions from the Heye Museum, Vol. XVII), 1960.

10 Charles Marius Barbeau, "Indian Days of the Western Prairies," *Bulletin of the National Museum of Canada*, No. 163, 1960, figure 28; Frederic H. Douglas and René d'Harnoncourt, *Indian Art of the United States*, New York, 1941, color-plate p. 24. Other examples of this type of hide are in the Denver Art Museum, the Wyoming State Museum, the Brooklyn Museum, Noble Hotel, Lander, Wyoming, etc.

11 Miss Mabel Morrow of Sante Fé, New Mexico is putting the finishing touches on a manuscript which will answer most of the questions about tribal styles in *parfleche* decoration.

12 See Ruth Underhill, *Pueblo Crafts*, Lawrence, 1944, for a detailed discussion of pottery types, and Frederic H. Douglas, *Modern Pueblo Pottery Types* (Denver Art Museum Leaflet No. 53–54), 1933.

13 Theodora Kroeber, *Ishi in Two Worlds*, Berkeley, 1961.

14 Leslie Spier and Edward Sapir, *Wishram Ethnography* (Publications in Anthropology, Vol. III, No. 3), 1930.

15 William N. Fenton, "Masked Medicine Societies of the Iroquois," *Annual Report of the Smithsonian Institution*, 1940, pp. 397–430.

Bibliography

The following bibliography is a brief listing of the more important books dealing with the artistic aspects of American Indian culture. It is not intended as an exhaustive list, but it is a guide to additional reading on specific subjects. A few of the books are included only because they are mentioned in the text. This bibliography has been updated to the present.

The literature on the American Indian is quite extensive, and fortunately there are excellent bibliographies available. For anyone interested in detailed information I can strongly recommend the first two works cited:

Harding, Anne D., and Bolling, Patricia. "Bibliography of North American Indian Art." Mimeographed, Washington, D.C. 1939. (Out of print; references listed by technique; a handy guide but outdated.)

Murdock, George P. *Ethnographic Bibliography of North America.* (Human Relations Area Files.) 3rd ed.; New Haven: Yale University Press, 1960. (A listing of references by tribe and area.)

Adair, John. *The Navaho and Pueblo Silversmiths.* Norman: University of Oklahoma Press, 1944.

American Indian Art: Form and Tradition. Catalogue of an exhibition organized by the Walker Art Center, the Indian Art Association, and the Minneapolis Institute of Arts, Minneapolis, 1972.

Amsden, Charles A. *Navaho Weaving.* Santa Ana, Calif.: The Fine Arts Press, 1934. (Chicago: Rio Grande Press, 1964.)

Appleton, Le Roy. *Indian Art of the Americas.* New York: Charles Scribner's Sons, 1950.

Art of the Northwest Coast. Catalogue of an exhibition at the Princeton University Art Museum, New Jersey, 1969.

Barbeau, Charles Marius. "Totem Poles," *Bulletin of the National Museum of Canada,* No. 119 (Anthropological Series, No. 30.) 2 vols. Ottawa, 1930.

———. "Haida Carvers in Argillite," *Bulletin of the National Museum of Canada,* No. 139. Ottawa, 1957.

———. "Indian Days of the Western Prairies," *Bulletin of the National Museum of Canada,* No. 163. Ottawa, 1960. (Good illustrations of pictographic painting, but text is a collection of myths.)

Barnett, Homer G. *The Coast Salish of British Columbia.* Eugene: University of Oregon Press, 1955.

Benndorf, Helga, and Speyer, Arthur. *Indianer Nordamerikas.* Offenbach: Deutsches Ledermuseum, 1968.

Berlandier, Jean Louis. *The Indians of Texas in 1830.* Edited by John C. Ewers. Washington, D.C.: Smithsonian Institution Press, 1969.

Birket-Smith, Kaj. *The Eskimos.* New York: E.P. Dutton & Co., Inc., 1936.

Bourke, John G. "Medicine-men of the Apache," *9th Annual Report of the Bureau of American Ethnology* (Washington, D.C., Smithsonian Institution), 1892.

Brody, J. J. *Indian Painters and White Patrons.* Albuquerque: University of New Mexico Press, 1971.

Bushnell, David I., Jr. *Drawings by George Gibbs in the Far Northwest, 1849–1851.* (Smithsonian Miscellaneous Collections, Vol. XCVII, No. 8.) Washington, D.C.: Government Printing Office, 1938. (A sketch of a canoe prow is reproduced in the text.)

Colton, Harold S. *Hopi Kachina Dolls.* Albuquerque: University of New Mexico Press, 1959.

Covarrubias, Miguel. *The Eagle, the Jaguar, and the Serpent.* New York: Alfred A. Knopf, 1954.

Davis, Robert T. *Native Arts of the Pacific Northwest.* Stanford: Stanford University Press, 1949.

Dockstader, Frederick J. "The Kachina and the White Man," *Cranbrook Institute of Science Bulletin,* No. 35. Bloomfield Hills, Mich., 1954.

———. *Indian Art in America.* Greenwich, Conn.: New York Graphic Society, 1961.

Donaldson, Thomas C. "The George Catlin Indian Gallery," *Annual Report of the United States National Museum* (Washington, D.C., Smithsonian Institution), 1885.

Dorsey, George A. *The Ponca Sun Dance.* (Field Columbian Museum Anthropological Series, Vol. VII, No. 2.) Chicago, 1905. (Complete discussion of this important Plains ceremony for one tribe.)

Douglas, Frederic H. *Modern Pueblo Pottery Types.* (Denver Art Museum Leaflet No. 53–54), 1933.

———, and d'Harnoncourt, René. *Indian Art of the United States.* New York: The Museum of Modern Art, 1941.

Drucker, Philip. *Indians of the Northwest Coast.* New York: Natural History Press, 1963. (An excellent and complete discussion of the people and art.)

Duff, Wilson. *The Indian History of British Columbia.* (Anthropology in British Columbia, Memoir, No. 5.) Provincial Museum of British Columbia, Victoria, 1964.

———; Holm, Bill; and Reid, Bill. *Arts of the Raven.* Vancouver, B.C.: Vancouver Art Gallery, 1967.

Dunn, Dorothy. "The Development of Modern American Indian Painting," *El Palacio* (Santa Fé, 1951), 331–53.

———. *American Indian Painting of the Southwest and the Plains Areas.* Albuquerque: University of New Mexico Press, 1968.